The Fourth WomanSleuth Anthology
Contemporary Mystery Stories by Women

Also edited by Irene Zahava

Anthologies
Finding Courage
Hear the Silence
Lesbian Love Stories
Lesbian Love Stories—Volume Two
Love, Struggle and Change
My Father's Daughter
My Mother's Daughter
Speaking for Ourselves
Through Other Eyes
Word of Mouth
Word of Mouth—Volume Two

The WomanSleuth Mystery Series
The WomanSleuth Anthology
The Second WomanSleuth Anthology
The Third WomanSleuth Anthology

Journals
Earth Songs
Moonflower
Water Spirit

The Fourth WomanSleuth Anthology
Contemporary Mystery Stories by Women

Edited by Irene Zahava

The Crossing Press
Freedom, California 95109

Library of Congress Cataloging-in-Publication Data
Irene Zahava
    The Fourth WomanSleuth anthology : contemporary mystery
    stories by women / edited by Irene Zahava.
        p.   cm.
Includes bibliographical references.
    ISBN 0-89594-522-3 (cloth). -- ISBN 0-89594-521-5 (paper)
    1. Detective and mystery stories, American. 2. American
fiction--Women authors. 3. Women detectives--Fiction.
PS648.D4F68 1991
813'.0872089287--dc20   91-22712
                                                                 CIP

Contents

The Pirtle Problem

Brenda Melton Burnham

Most everyone in Rocky Falls knew Floyd Pirtle had a tendency to wander and that recently he'd been wandering in the direction of Melba Wheatley. Whether Edna Pirtle or Herb Wheatley were among those who knew was cause for conjecture. The consensus of opinion at Ida Schwartz's Pink Poodle Hair Salon where I worked was that they did.

"How could Edna not know?" Gloria Peabody exclaimed. "Floyd's been chasing around for thirty years, for gosh sakes! Practically since they got back from their honeymoon."

"Some women are so dense," Martha Hightower snorted. "If I ever caught Albert doing something like that, I can assure you he wouldn't be able to again."

There were nods of agreement all round.

"Edna's pretty distracted now," Millie Coughlin threw in, "what with her mother's death last year and her dad not being well. It could be she doesn't know about Melba."

"That Vern," Martha scoffed at the mention of Edna's dad. "At his age he should be worn out. He gave Flo a hard time, you know. Like mother, like daughter; both of 'em picked womanizers. I tell you, if you allow it, you deserve it." Her point made, she pulled the hood of the dryer back over her head.

Ida, who was putting a color rinse on Gloria's hair, said, "Herb's the one I worry about. He's meaner'n a two-headed snake."

"Remember when Buster Martin came sniffing around Melba a couple of years ago?" Bertha Mull chuckled. "Herb like to killed him." She took the mirror I handed her and checked the back of her hair. "You don't think it's too short, do you Gladys?"

I assured her it wasn't. Besides, it was too late anyway; I'd already cut it.

"I thought Floyd was seeing Alice Beaudry," Millie remarked.

"Heavens, no." Gloria lowered her voice to a dramatic whisper. "Didn't you hear? They had a big scene at the Grange dance two weeks ago and that was the end of that. Floyd don't like women that make trouble."

"I just can't understand how Edna . . . "

The bell tinkled as the front door opened and Edna Pirtle came in.

"Hello there, Edna," Ida greeted her loudly. "What a pretty blouse. Is it new?"

Edna, a mouse of a woman, slipped her jacket off and hung it on the rack. "Thank you. Floyd bought it for me."

Everyone had some favorable comment to make. A lengthy conversation on fashion followed and the awkward moment was gone.

In the next two weeks the rumors about Floyd and Melba grew. Some folks claimed they were planning to run away together; others said Melba was still playing hard to get.

Then one noon-hour my husband Bill—he's one of the three full-time policemen in Rocky Falls—came home and announced, "Floyd Pirtle was shot to death sometime last night."

I was cutting his sandwich at the time and nearly sliced my finger off. "You're kidding!"

Bill poured himself a cup of coffee and sat down. "Not likely. Arnie Hooper found the body at Floyd's cabin. Arnie'd gone up to the lake to do a little fishing and saw Floyd's car there. Went over to chat and surprise, surprise."

"How awful."

"You got that right. Shotgun. Both barrels."

I shuddered. "I don't suppose it was a . . . ?"

"An accident? Hardly. Unless you think Floyd got up afterwards and got rid of the gun somehow. And believe me, honey, Floyd didn't get up. Nope. Somebody wanted him thoroughly dead."

"Do you have any idea who did it?"

"No Gladys, we don't. But it doesn't appear we need your help right now, thanks." Bill grinned, so I knew he was kidding. After all, I had helped a couple of times before.

He didn't tell me not to get involved, though. He probably knew it wouldn't do any good.

Floyd's murder was quite naturally the main topic of conversation at the Pink Poodle for the next few days.

"I can't imagine Edna doing a thing like that," Bertha Hull said while I was setting her hair.

"What makes you think Edna did it?"

"I didn't say that now, did I?" she snapped. "But he was fooling around on her."

"Herb did it," Gloria Peabody stated emphatically. "I should think that's obvious. He's always been a violent man, everyone knows that. Of course, Floyd was asking for it."

"What about Alice Beaudry?" Ida suggested. "I heard she was mighty jealous when Floyd dumped her for Melba."

"Bill didn't tell you who they suspect?" Bertha asked me.

I shook my head. Bill knows he can trust me not to repeat anything. He also knows I hear a lot over the brushes and the curlers.

The next morning I dropped by the bakery on my way to work, to pick up some cinnamon rolls for Ida and me—not that either of us needed them. But Alice Beaudry worked at the bakery and cinnamon rolls seemed as good a reason as any to drop by and chat.

I had to dawdle a bit (I told Lucy Watkins when she came to wait on me that I was still making up my mind) before Alice was free from her other customers. While I got my wallet out I said, so only she could hear, "A terrible thing about Floyd Pirtle."

Alice rolled the top of the sack down tightly and dropped it on the counter.

"It must've been an awful shock for you," I continued.

She took the ten I handed her, flung the change down and turned away, but not before I saw the smudged mascara under her eyes. Embarrassed and ashamed, I stuffed the money in my sweater pocket and hurried out.

When I stopped by Perkin's Market after work I practically ran Vern Hadley over with my shopping cart.

"How's Edna doing?" I asked, taking advantage of the situation.

"She's mighty upset." He put three apples in a plastic bag and placed them in his basket. "She'll make it, though."

Vern had always been a big man, but since his wife's death he had grown lean. Now his nose and cheekbones jutted like rocks from the granite cliff of his face.

"With no children to comfort her it's a good thing she has you," I said. "I suppose she doesn't like to fish and that's why she didn't go with Floyd up to the cabin that night."

"She was with me," Vern practically shouted. "The whole evening. Everybody's trying to make out like Edna killed the man and it's not true. Just because your husband's a policeman don't give you rights, young lady." He maneuvered his cart around me and pushed it down the aisle toward the canned vegetables.

I smiled at Bertha Mull, who was standing by the potato bin, listening, then I headed for the dairy section. Twice up to bat and two strike-outs, I thought.

That night, after the kids had gone to bed and we were watching the late news, Bill said, "Who've the ladies at the Pink Poodle picked as the prime suspect in Floyd's murder?"

"It's a toss-up between Edna, Herb Wheatley and Alice Beaudry. The ones who think Edna did it feel she was justified, while the Herb-accusers figure it's because he has a mean streak anyway. The Alice group gives her no defense at all, since she didn't have any business fooling around with a married man in the first place."

When Bill didn't comment I continued. "I stopped by the bakery this morning and spoke to Alice for a minute. I think she really cared for Floyd."

That got me a sideways look. I put my mending down and asked him point-blank, "Who do you think did it?"

"Don't know. Alice was home, alone, all evening. Edna says she took some of the apple pie she'd baked over to her father after Floyd left around seven. Vern swears she stayed late to watch a TV special."

"So I heard."

Bill ignored the interruption. "Melba was alone, too, since Herb was at the Moosehead Tavern 'til they closed, drinking beer and shooting off his mouth."

"About anything in particular?"

"About Floyd's attentions to Melba, as a matter of fact, and what he'd do to Floyd if he caught him at it."

I picked up the pair of jeans that I'd been patching. "A little obvious then, isn't it, when Floyd is found dead the next morning?"

Bill shut off the TV. "That's my argument exactly. Plus the fact that Herb was pretty well crocked. And that he exchanged a few punches afterwards with Butch Cogwell over who bagged the largest elk last hunting season."

"In other words he had a chance to work off some of his anger?"

"That's what I figure. Actually, nobody has an alibi, since the county coroner can't pinpoint the exact time of death. The idiot has trouble telling *if* a person's dead, let alone *when*. Anyway, the Chief's sure Herb's the one, so you know what that means."

I did. Once Chief Wilson makes up his mind, there's no changing it. "What about the gun? What about fingerprints?"

"We searched the grounds and dragged the section of lake near the cabin. Nothing. In this county everybody's got a shotgun or two. The killer could have taken it home with him and who's to know? As for fingerprints, practically all the surfaces in the cabin had been wiped clean." He shrugged his shoulders tiredly and turned the TV back on.

The next day was my day off, so I made some turkey and homemade noodles and dropped over to express my sympathy to Edna.

"Gladys, how thoughtful of you," she said at the door. I said the usual "it was nothing" and added my condolences. When a sharp breeze whipped past I took advantage of it to pull my jacket tighter around me.

"Won't you come in?"

"Well, just for a minute," I assured her, my goal achieved.

She led me back to the kitchen and poured coffee for us, then we sat and stared into our cups as if we could read the future there.

"I know a lot of people think Floyd wasn't a good husband to me," Edna said softly to her coffee. "But that's not true. He was."

"Of course he was," I agreed, not believing it.

"And he loved me. He always loved me."

Having committed myself to one small lie, I embarked on another. "Of course he did." Heck, maybe he did, for all I knew.

She began to sob, head bent over the table, shoulders shaking.

I felt a definite twinge of guilt.

"Oh my God, Gladys, what am I going to do? Mom's gone, now Floyd, and Dad's not well. I'll have no one . . . no one." She blew her nose fiercely and shoved the tissue in her pocket.

I reached out and patted her hand, uncomfortable as always in the presence of grief. There was nothing more constructive I could do here—for myself or Edna—so I left and went home.

"I'm sure she didn't do it," I told Bill later, when we were going to bed. "She's one of those people who let others shape their lives for them. It would never occur to her to take action."

"The jails are full of victims who did take action, Gladys." He fluffed up his pillow, punched his fist into it and leaned back, satisfied.

I couldn't think of a good response, so I turned off the bed-lamp and kissed him goodnight. His point was well-taken, alright. I just didn't agree with him.

Melba Wheatley wore her hair hanging down her back—not a style I find particularly attractive on teenagers, let alone thirty-some-year-old women—so she wasn't a Pink Poodle customer. I had to drop by the hardware store where she clerked to get a word with her.

Under normal conditions most folks would say she was a pretty woman. Today her nose seemed sharper and there were dark shadows under her eyes. Above the collar of the high-necked dress I thought I saw the edge of a dark bruise.

"I'm looking for some wallpaper for the bedroom," I told her, "but I'm not sure what I want."

While she talked wallpaper I talked Floyd. "This must be awful for you," I said, my fingers testing a sample.

"Folks act like I don't have feelings at all." Her hands sorted through the little paper scraps.

"They don't mean to be unkind."

"Ha. They love it. They love to see somebody miserable, so's they can stand around and make judgments on 'em."

"This is a nice pattern. Do you have it in mauve? How's Herb handling the situation?"

"No, these are the only colors. But there's a nice mauve over here." She moved to another display. "Herb'll do just fine as long as he's got his drinking buddies and someone to fight with when he gets riled. God knows he's getting enough fights lately to keep his fists off . . . " Her words trailed to a halt. Her hands moved quickly, shifting this, rejecting that. "Here's one you might like."

I left without buying a thing.

Bill was going to work late that evening; the kids all had after-school activities. I put my casserole in the oven, then sat at the kitchen table and thought about the women in Floyd Pirtle's life.

Edna, Melba, Alice. All victims in their way. If it'd been me, I wouldn't have let Floyd Pirtle past my front door—except to fix the plumbing, which he was good at, heaven knows.

As for Herb Wheatley, he was a bully, no doubt about it. But pumping both barrels into a man, face to face? That wasn't the action of a bully.

No, the answer lay in the personalities of the women. I was sure of it.

The newspaper landed on the front porch with a thud and I went to bring it in. With everybody else gone, I'd get first shot at it for a change. I'd read the whole front section and turned to the TV listings before I got my brilliant idea. I grabbed my sweater and dashed out the back door, eager to prove my theory. Since the sun was still out I decided to walk.

Edna wasn't home, so I headed over to the old Hadley place. They were both there, father and daughter; Vern leaning back in his recliner, Edna huddled on the couch.

"I just dropped by to see how you were doing," I prattled. "Boy, I'll be glad when warm weather arrives, won't you? March is such a silly month, neither winter nor spring."

Vern grunted. Edna huddled.

"Anything good on TV?"

No response.

I didn't let their lack of enthusiasm stop me. "You know, we missed that TV special last week about the Brazilian rain forest. Amy could've used some of the information to complete her term paper, but she went with the Pep Squad over to Rayville for the game and forgot all about it. Teenagers are so irresponsible, aren't they?"

Edna and Vern stared at me like I was drunk or something.

"Well, anyway, I'd heard you watched it, the special I mean, and I was wondering if you could answer a couple of questions about it? I should let Amy take her lumps I suppose, but you know how mothers are."

"I haven't the foggiest idea what you're talking about," Edna replied when I finally shut up.

"Sure, you remember," Vern interrupted. "That's what we watched the night . . . that night."

"Oh, of course," his daughter agreed quickly. "How silly of me. I'm sorry, Gladys, with all that's happened since then, well, you understand."

I said, very gently, "You didn't see it at all, did you Edna? Vern just said you were here to provide you with an alibi."

"An alibi? What would I need an alibi for? I didn't . . . I wouldn't have harmed Floyd." The amazement on her face was duplicated on her father's.

"But . . . you were so unhappy that night," he stammered when she turned to him. "And you got up and left so sudden-like . . . ."

"You thought I drove out to the lake and killed him?"

Vern didn't answer.

"Oh my heavens." Edna rubbed her eyes. "I was upset. I needed to talk to someone. But you looked so tired and I didn't want to worry you, so I left. I drove around for awhile, then went to the church. I thought maybe praying would help—although it hadn't so far. I'd been praying and praying, you know, and nothing had changed.

"Then Father Shay came in. He asked if there was anything he could do to help and, well, I ended up crying on his shoulder for what seemed like hours."

"You didn't go out to the cabin at all?" Vern demanded.

"Of course not. I hated the cabin, you know that. I never went there."

"But *you* did, didn't you?" I said to Vern. "You and Floyd have always taken care of Edna in your way, haven't you? Only now you're getting older. Did you start wondering if Floyd would continue to care for her as well as you thought he should?"

His gnarled hands clutched his denim-covered thighs tightly; he didn't speak for a while. When he did, the words came out harshly in the quiet room. "Doc Leatherby told me three weeks ago I got cancer." Edna started to interrupt, but Vern waved her silent. "I couldn't help worrying. All the talk . . . well, I could see what it'd be like for her after I'm gone. I couldn't let that happen now, could I?"

"Daddy!" Edna went to crouch by the recliner.

"Good Lord, girl, I didn't kill him. When I got there someone had already done for him." Vern released his pants leg and clumsily patted his daughter's arm. With the other hand he covered his eyes, as if to blot out a memory. "What a mess. You've no idea. And the gun lyin' right there by the door. I guess I wasn't thinking too clearly by that time. All I could see was you rushing out of the house here . . ."

I helped him out. "So you cleaned up?"

He nodded. "I wiped the place down. The door, the table, whatever I thought she might've touched. Took the gun and drove all the way around to the bluff on the other side and tossed it in the lake. I figured they wouldn't bother to drag the whole thing. Too damn big. Not logical."

When he stopped I said, "You've both behaved very foolishly," as if they were my kids. "I think you ought to call Bill right away, don't you?"

I left after making sure Vern was dialing the police station. I'd been sure he was lying about something, although I hadn't known what. His explanation had at least cleared up a few of my questions.

Outside, dusk had fallen and a cold wind was blowing. I pulled my sweater closer around my neck and shoved my hands in the pockets.

I was pretty sure I knew who had killed Floyd, but there was one more person to talk to first. If things had happened as I thought . . . well, now seemed as good a time as any to check it out.

Melba opened the door a crack in response to my knock.

"Is Herb home?" I asked.

She shook her head.

"Good. I wanted to talk to you anyway. Can I come in?"

She just stood there, peering out at me. When it seemed she wasn't going to let me in I decided to go ahead and conduct my investigation from the stoop.

"The night Floyd was killed . . ." I saw her shudder, but good manners weren't on my agenda at the moment. ". . . you were supposed to meet him at the cabin, weren't you?"

Melba's head disappeared and, after a second, the door swung wide open.

"Come in, Gladys," Alice said. Since she had a pistol practically glued to Melba's left ear I decided I would.

"Alice," I said with a big smile. "How handy you should be here. I was coming to see you next. You really were the only logical one I could come up with to have killed Floyd."

"You're such a busybody," she exclaimed, slamming our escape hatch shut behind us with a bang. "Both of you, sit on the couch."

Melba and I did as we were told, like good little hostages. Alice stood about six feet away, smiling at us.

"Let's see now, where was I? Oh yes, I was just telling Melba how sorry I was she didn't go to the cabin. Well, I wasn't sorry at the time. I was glad. Glad because then I had Floyd all to myself." She swallowed and the smile left her face. "But he didn't want me. He made that perfectly clear. He said I bored him. Bored him! He said he didn't like his women too easy, that the fun was in the chase.

"I told him I loved him and he laughed. You would've liked that, wouldn't you, Melba? His shotgun was right there, leaning against the wall. I grabbed it." She paused for a moment, perhaps remembering. "You know what he did? He laughed again. He said I didn't have the guts to shoot." She made a funny sound, half-sob, half-chuckle, deep in her throat.

"Why would you want to harm Melba?" I asked, quite calmly I thought, considering the circumstances. "It wasn't her fault . . . "

"She's got a husband. Edna's got sympathy. And what do I have? Nothing!" She screamed out the last word, then, in yet another abrupt mood change, her face took on that distant look it had worn before. I wasn't sure which was the more frightening. "I've been thinking about that the last few days and I decided Melba hasn't suffered enough. No, not nearly enough."

On the couch beside me Melba twitched. I don't know what she was thinking, but I was trying to come up with some idea of how I could gain the upper hand, let alone the gun.

When the front door opened with a bang and a curse, all three of us were startled. As Alice half-turned at the interruption I pushed myself off the sofa.

Still in a half-crouch, I ran at her, shouting, "Look out. She's got a gun."

My head hit her in the mid-section. The gun fired. Alice and I fell to the floor. Melba shrieked. Herb Wheatley yelled, "What the hell?"

"Get the gun. Get the gun," I called out, straddling Alice the same way I used to do to so many others back in my tomboy days. It's amazing how some skills are never quite forgotten.

Herb leaned against the wall, white as an altar cloth, useless in his shock. Surprisingly, it was his wife who jumped to my assistance. Melba wrenched the weapon from Alice's hand while I held her arms down.

"Call Vern Hadley's house," I said. "Bill should be there by now." Thank heavens I'd stayed at the Hadley house long enough to hear Vern ask to speak to Bill. Not that I didn't trust Vern, of course.

Herb still didn't move. Melba walked to the phone, holding Alice at gunpoint the whole time.

Some hours later, after all the excitement was over, Bill and I sat at our kitchen table, finishing the last of our coffee.

"Poor Alice," I commented as I stood up to put the cups on the counter. "Poor Melba. Poor Edna. All this because they chose the wrong man to love."

"Lucky ole you," Bill said, patting my fanny as I went by.

"My, my, my." I grinned. "And it looks like I'm about to get luckier, right?"

Emma Twiggs to the Rescue

Helen and Lorri Carpenter

"Can you find the way back to Otter Creek, Jim?" Emma Twiggs asked.

The septuagenarian sleuth kept her voice cheerful as Nancy Barnes, Galveston Investigations' matchless secretary, helped her into the small boat.

James Galveston, owner of the detective firm that bore his name (and was the source of most of the trio's misadventures), answered sourly, "I don't know, but I'm going to try. Twelve hours of surveillance on this island is enough." He took the middle seat facing Nancy and started to row.

Emma peered ahead. A wall of moist, white fog lay over the water, closing them in. Drifting in a swamp in the middle of the night was definitely a damp experience. I bet Jim's wishing I'd learn to keep my mouth shut, the sleuth thought wryly.

Her mind returned to the fateful Monday just two days before, when Nancy had called the office to extend her Florida vacation.

"I'm staying in Blue Sky." Nancy's voice had been firm. "There are strange lights and odd noises on the islands near Dad's home, and I'm not leaving until I find out what they are."

"Galveston Investigations to the rescue?" Emma had offered.

Nancy's laugh was short and sweet. "I wish you were here, Em, but Jim and Blue Sky would definitely not mix."

"Look," Emma had answered in a tone she knew would prevail,

"I cannot stand to have him in the office for another week. The database will be ruined—you can't imagine the problems he's already caused."

The naked truth worked. Nancy promptly gave in. Selling the trip to Jim took a little longer. As soon as Emma mentioned Florida he eyed her suspiciously.

"Is this a trick to get me to take a vacation, Aunty?"

"Of course not, Jimbo," Emma said sweetly. "I'm sure Nancy can investigate quite well on her own."

Her logic brought him around immediately. "Book two reservations on the next flight," he said. "I'm going over to Safari Anywhere and warm up my charge card."

No wonder he's unhappy, Emma mused, as her thoughts returned to the present. Not a single odd occurrence since we arrived, and no place but a swamp to wear all the clothes he bought.

She glanced at her nephew. His well-groomed, carefully maintained good looks—along with his tan safari pants and crisp shirt—had gone limp in the misty air.

"Damn," Jim muttered under his breath.

The mild expletive prompted Emma to smile. From her years spent raising him she knew rowing a boat wasn't one of his favorite pastimes. "Maybe we should float with the current," she suggested.

Jim scowled. "Are you saying I can't captain this craft?"

Even as he spoke, the bottom of the small wooden boat bumped once and stopped, stuck on a sandbar.

Emma, following Nancy's lead, chose silence as her best alternative, and merely watched his health-club-cultivated muscles bulge as he used an oar to shove them off. The rowboat broke free and continued its slow drift downstream. Only the sound of water dripping off the raised oars broke the ghostly calm.

Emma, sensing no forgiveness in her nephew's features, turned her thoughts to Nancy's father and the mystery at hand. Alvin Barnes was another impossible man. From the moment she'd stepped off the plane, the sexagenarian had been trying to get her alone.

So far she'd managed to stay one step ahead of him by keeping Nancy and Jim within hearing distance. At the same time she'd gleaned bits and pieces of the mysterious happenings on the swamp's deserted islands. Far better to thwart his advances by engaging him in small talk than embarrass Nancy by giving him the karate chop he so richly deserved. At sixty-eight, Alvin Barnes apparently believed he was God's gift to women.

Even as the pleasing image of Alvin sprawled at her feet crossed her mind, Emma saw a beam of light ooze through the fog. She leaned forward and pointed. Jim dipped the oars and swung the boat in the direction she indicated. Low-hanging tree branches scraped against the wooden frame. Nancy, ever efficient, grabbed a sturdy limb and pulled them into the sloped, marshy bank. Reaching for the bow rope, she anchored the craft to a bush.

The thick white mist cloaking the water thinned to a filmy vapor over higher ground, making the dry land of the island stand up like a pimple on the face of the water. Emma stayed in her seat while Jim stood and peered through the thick brush.

"The light's moving, as if someone's pacing back and forth," he said in a low voice.

Before Emma could rise to see what he was talking about, she heard a heavy rumble. "Is that a truck?"

"Something isn't right," Nancy whispered. "There shouldn't be any vehicles on this island. The bridge isn't safe—it's been closed for months."

"I'm going to investigate. I want both of you to stay here." Jim jumped to the bank and disappeared into the dense foliage that seemed to grow everywhere in this part of Florida.

The minute he was out of sight, Emma turned to Nancy. "Jim may need me. If we aren't back in ten minutes, go for help."

Without waiting for Nancy's agreement, the sleuth stepped to the marshy bank, pushed aside the entwining branches and pressed forward. She'd gone only a few yards when she saw headlights slash through the trees.

Emma dropped to the ground as a long, slat-sided truck swung into the clearing. When the engine died, a shaggy-haired man emerged from the cab. He was followed by a tall, wiry youth with rolled up shirt sleeves—and right behind him came a grizzled giant, carrying a rifle.

Where was Jim? Emma scanned the area and saw him crouched behind a tree. As she started to crawl toward her nephew, the huge sumo wrestler-shaped man raised and cocked his weapon. "Come out of there with your hands up!" he growled.

Emma glanced at her nephew, then at his opponent. She saw

Jim hesitate before he moved forward, his hands above his head. The other two men, following orders from the rifle-toting giant, grabbed his upraised arms and dragged him to the truck. Without another word, the behemoth swung the gun in a semi-circular arch. As the blow landed, Jim crumpled to the ground.

Emma shrieked in outrage. Any thought of her own safety vanished as she jumped to her feet and rushed to Jim's aid. She had no idea what impression the abrupt emergence of her five-foot-two-inch, thistle-haired frame made on the men, but for the space of one unsteady heartbeat, all three simply stared at her.

"The old lady's seen too much," the giant said. "We'll have to take care of her, too."

"My pleasure," a familiar voice said.

Emma turned and saw Alvin Barnes step around the side of the truck. He grinned wickedly and clamped a hand over her arm, effectively stopping her from running away. As the sleuth kicked him, the other men grabbed her legs. When she opened her mouth to scream, the tall youth towered over her, fist raised menacingly. "Shut up . . . or else," he snarled.

Unwilling to find out how far he'd go, Emma pressed her lips together. As the men lowered her to the ground, she glanced at Jim, who lay still as a stone less than three feet away. She fervently wished he'd come to. Maybe together they could discover what the three men and Alvin were doing in the swamp.

Her mind flickered to Nancy. Since her young friend hadn't appeared, Emma could only hope she'd gone for help . . . and did not yet know of her father's duplicity.

The idea of having to tell Nancy of Alvin's despicable behavior made her heart ache. Think of something else, she told herself. Concentrate on rescuing Jim and getting out of here safely.

But before her mind could formulate a plan of action, Alvin Barnes brandished a rope. He quickly wrapped the rough twine around her wrists and ankles.

"That should hold her," he said.

"Too bad we can't shoot them both," the overgrown ox with the rifle remarked. His eyes glinted with disappointment.

"Don't be stupid," Alvin Barnes said. "I told you the gun's for alligators, and even then only in an emergency. A shot might be heard. We don't want the cops out here."

"She could have friends," the shaggy-haired man said.

Emma caught her breath. Alvin knew Nancy was in the swamp with them tonight. Would he betray his own daughter?

Alvin merely shook his head. "If you're worried, let's drive to the other site."

"Good idea," the tall one agreed. "I'll get a rope for the guy. We'll take him and the snoopy broad with us. We can drop them there. Give the 'gators a feast."

"I think we should leave them here." Alvin Barnes stared at Emma speculatively.

The sleuth could imagine what was in his mind. As surely as she was lying with her face in the soft mud of the swamp, this man could not let her or Jim live without exposing himself.

"No." The giant who'd attacked Jim regained his attitude of leadership. "She might untie herself and get away."

He bent over, picked Emma up, and heaved her into the truck bed. She landed on her tailbone beside an assortment of metal containers. A second later Jim was tossed in. Then the truck doors slammed and the engine roared to life.

As the heavy vehicle bounced down the rough trail, Emma managed to work herself into a sitting position. The new posture eased the dull ache developing in her back, and brought her closer to Jim, but did little for her troubled thoughts.

Silent tears slid down her cheeks. She closed her eyes and pressed against one of the hard containers that imprisoned her as effectively as a cage. Never in her life had she been so afraid. Her stomach was churning, and everything she'd eaten for dinner—just a few hours before, sitting across the table from a smiling Alvin Barnes—seemed about to come up. A foul odor filled her nose.

She shifted position and the stench grew stronger. Turning slightly, she saw the drum behind her was leaking. Where the rivulets of liquid had run the paint was blistered.

Panic seized her. She rolled over. Away from the drums the night air was sharp and fresh. She took a deep breath, then another. When her head began to clear, she braced herself against the side wall and used her feet to shove Jim away from the oozing substance. No wonder he was still unconscious. The fumes were thick enough to choke a horse. As she eyed the barrels, wondering about their contents, the truck skidded to a halt.

A moment later the tailgate dropped open. Emma, half-leaning against it, fell into the arms of Alvin Barnes. He carried her to the edge of the woods and set her down against a tree.

He seemed about to say something when the other three men approached, hauling Jim between them. Alvin straightened and spoke to them instead. "They'll be all right here until we're finished."

Emma watched the trio drop Jim to the ground. She trembled, and Alvin shifted his gaze. "Don't worry," he drawled, his dark eyes unreadable. "It'll be over soon."

"Come on, Barnes, give us a hand with the barrels. We want to get out of this mud hole tonight," the shaggy-haired man snapped.

As Alvin and his cohorts walked back to the truck, Emma knew she had to escape. The rational thought pushed her fear away and let her training take charge.

The first step was to untie herself. Using a sawing motion, she rubbed her bonds against the rough bark of the tree. Within minutes her skin was raw, but her hands were free. She undid the ropes that bound her ankles next, then turned her attention to the men and their activities.

Aided by the bright moonlight, Emma saw they'd unloaded all the barrels. As they began rolling them, one by one, toward a nearby stand of tall cypress trees, she noticed dozens of other drums lying in haphazard fashion all over the marshy ground.

An illegal dump site! Of course! She should have realized—would have realized—if she hadn't been so concerned about getting safely out of the swamp.

Emma watched the foursome wrestle with the recalcitrant metal vats for several minutes while she considered and rejected different courses of action. Finally, after a quick check to make sure Jim was all right, she crept to the truck.

Concealed behind the vehicle's oversized front tire she unscrewed the valve cap. Using it as a tool, she loosened the valve stem. Hopefully the resulting slow leak would stop the truck before it left the swamp. Just to be sure, Emma moved to the rear wheel and repeated the process.

As she was about to flee back to Jim, Emma saw the men, their nefarious task completed, stride into the clearing.

"Do you have my money?" she heard Alvin say.

The sleuth knew if they spotted her she was finished. Heart pounding like a boom-box on high volume, she eased toward the open tailgate.

She reached the protective overhang just as the large-sized leader snapped, "Got your payoff right here, Barnes."

His unfriendly tone was followed by a roundhouse right that landed squarely on Alvin's chin.

As Nancy's father sagged to the ground, the tall, shirtsleeved youth laughed sardonically. "That'll teach him to be greedy."

"We'll leave the jerk here," the giant said. A mocking smile played at the corners of his mouth. "He's in over his head. He won't tell the cops a thing."

He stepped across Alvin's inert form and climbed into the truck. "You two get the old lady and her friend," he ordered as he started the engine. "We'll dump them where they'll never be found."

Emma shivered. In a moment they would discover she was gone. Then what?

As the duo headed toward her nephew, Emma, using the tailgate as a handhold, pushed herself upright. She was almost standing when a gleam of metal caught her eye.

The rifle! Goliath must have left it in the back of the truck while he moved the drums. She lifted the weapon and checked to make sure it was loaded. She hadn't fired a rifle in years, but somehow she knew she could.

Releasing the safety, she raised the firearm to her shoulder, stepped away from the truck, and in a voice filled with long-suppressed rage yelled, "Stop where you are!"

The two men nearest Jim halted in mid-stride, but the big man in the truck ignored her shouted order. He jammed the engine in gear and, wheels churning mud, skidded away into the night.

Emma held the gun steady and eyed the two men he'd left behind. "Don't move," she warned.

"We won't, lady. Please don't shoot," the tall youth pleaded. As he spoke his gaze shifted to a point over her left shoulder.

Alvin! Emma turned quickly and found herself staring into his narrow face.

"Take it easy, Emma," Alvin said. "I'm working with the sheriff."

His words didn't convince her. Even though his buddies had turned on him, Alvin needed to get her out of the way so she couldn't tell the authorities—or Nancy—what he'd been doing. She pressed her finger more tightly against the trigger. "Put your hands up," she ordered.

"Okay, Emma," he acceded, then added stubbornly, "But I wish you'd believe me."

He was still insisting he was on her side when Emma heard a police siren cut through the night air. At the same moment, but from another direction, Nancy stepped into the clearing.

Fifteen minutes later, Emma, Jim and Nancy listened in amazement as the sheriff recounted Alvin's role in the undercover operation.

"About a month ago, Alvin noticed strange lights on the island. The next day he found the first bunch of barrels. When he informed me, we decided he should pose as a greedy landowner who was willing to let his property be used for an illegal dump."

"For a fee, of course," Alvin added.

"Why didn't you tell me what you were involved in?" Nancy asked.

"I was afraid you'd worry," Alvin said. "I tried to confide in Emma, but I never could get her alone."

The sleuth remembered the karate chop she'd wanted to give Alvin when she thought he was making advances. Thank heavens she'd exercised restraint.

She smiled at him, and he looked at her admiringly. "One of the deputies wondered who unscrewed the valve stems," he said. "You're a quick thinker, Emma. I . . ."

"Please don't heap accolades on her," Jim interjected. "She displayed a definite lack of perception."

Emma flashed him a disbelieving glance. "What?"

The creases around Jim's mouth deepened, suggesting amusement. "Aunty, we both know you should have gone for help as soon as you saw me acting like I was unconscious."

The sleuth contemplated his soggy clothes and rumpled appearance. "If that was acting, Jimbo," she said to her favorite relative, "I nominate you for an Oscar."

A Little Yarn

Linda E. Clopton

Nell Byrd was a gossipy old woman who did nasty little needlepoints and gave them to folks who wanted them least. Sounds harmless enough, you might say. Not neighborly but harmless. That's what I thought, too, in the beginning.

Now not much happens in a place like Bradbury. The law, that's me and Uncle Rankin, has to break up a fight every now and then over at Jeeter's Place but, all in all, it's a quiet little town.

I used to think it was too quiet and shocked the Ladies Literary Society by running off to Atlanta and joining the police force. Turned out they didn't mind the career choice but thought the uniforms were tacky. Still, I did okay by myself. When I hit detective grade I learned to sniff out crime better than the canine corps. It got so they called me "the Nose," which was a lot better than "the hick chick."

But ten years in the city convinced me it's no place for a country girl, and I shocked the local matrons even more by coming home to Bradbury still single. I signed on with Uncle Rankin and the only thing tickling my nose was the ragweed until I heard what Nell Byrd was up to. It had been so long since I'd sniffed out any heavy deeds, three years by then, that I didn't pay much attention at first. Thought it was hay fever.

Now in a place the size of Bradbury everybody knows everybody by sight or by name. The Byrds were old money around these parts. He was a mite dandified but as nice and sober as she was ornery. A round, pink little man with a full crop of hair, pin-striped suits and polished shoes, he was what my daddy used to call "the gentry." Not his wife, though. When pushed, people called her a few other names.

I should have known something was brewing when I heard about Nell's gift to Sadie Miller. Sadie's a fine woman, but her boy Tommy's been a trial from the day he was born. Started on the weed in sixth grade and went on from there, though nobody's caught him yet. Well, Sadie got this pillow and it was all greens and browns with a repeated leaf pattern. Poor lady, innocent as Sunday morning she is. Damned if she didn't put that pillow right smack on her sofa for all the world to see 'til Tommy got home from one of his mysterious trips and spotted it.

My nose started to tickle when I heard about Sadie, but it was spring and lots of folk were sniffling and, like I said, it'd been a long time.

The next victim was Clara Lou Stokes. At their big anniversary shindig Clara Lou unwrapped a framed needlepoint and nearly passed out in the sweet potato pie. The picture was a four-poster with three heads on the pillows: a blonde (that's Clara Lou), a man with a mustache, and a flaming redhead. Ed Stokes and his secretary hadn't been discreet.

Old Collins the banker got one of Nell's presents, too. Showed a man at a desk piled with money and some of it peeking out of his bulging pockets. Lots of folks laughed but some of them transferred their accounts to Dawkinsville.

Nell even insulted her own cook. Mr. Byrd tried to reason with her over that one. Cousin Emily used to clean for the Byrds—Nell's hand never did fit a dusting rag—and she had a ringside seat. It seems the cook got pretty riled and went to Mr. Byrd in a huff, throwing a pillow at his feet and her "I quit" in his face. On the pillow a yarn cat flipped sand over a lopsided souffle.

Now Bernard Byrd has a soft voice, not that anybody gets to hear it much, but he raised it a little on that occasion. A gentleman as always, Emily said, but he tried. "You know how difficult it is to find help, my love, and this does show rather poor taste," Mr. Byrd said, stroking his cowlick nervously.

"So do her souffles," Nell snapped back. It seemed she was willing to sacrifice most anything for the sake of her hobby. You might say she enjoyed needling people.

Funny thing was, nobody complained. I reckon when there's fire it doesn't do any good to deny the smoke. I tell you what—there were enough stiff upper lips around here to rival the Miami morgue.

With nobody crying foul, I guess Nell got reckless, but she sure bit off more than she could chew when she took on Lettie Amberson. Lettie's never been one to sit back and let people walk over her. So when Nell gave her a pillow sporting a big fuchsia 46, Lettie, who's been thirty-nine for years, didn't wait twenty-four hours to strike back.

The very next morning while Nell sat under the dryer at Beth Ann's Beauty Boutique, helpless as a fish in a bucket, she got a package from Belk's. Under the wrappings she found a girdle. Top of the line, extra large, and heavy duty. Beth Ann couldn't hardly stop laughing long enough to tell me about it.

Emily heard about that one, too. Nell raged for ten minutes that evening, demanding that Mr. Byrd do something, but he avoided her eyes by studying himself in the mantel mirror and just asked, "What can I do? She's a generous woman. Tell me, dear, do you think I should change my part to the other side?"

"She's not generous. She's a bitch."

Emily was taken back by that kind of language in a fine household but, like I told her, scratch a rich person and you'll find the same kind of animal underneath as the rest of us. Anyhow, Nell's needle must have burned the canvas 'cause in just two days she finished another picture: a worn-out looking female dog. It had Lettie's head all right, vivid blond curls with dark roots. It arrived, special delivery, during Lettie's bridge club.

After that the flow of insults got swifter and deeper and gave folks plenty to talk about. Mr. Byrd and Emily tried to distract Nell with plans for his birthday dinner or the State Fair arts and crafts competition, but nothing changed her course for long. "As single-minded as a cat at a mouse hole," Emily said.

We all began to think Nell and Lettie were enjoying their feud until one day Mr. Byrd came home to find his wife dead. When we got his call up at the station, we made it to the scene in three minutes flat. Only time I've run the red light since we got it. Mr. Byrd looked shaky and I could've used a drink myself. Nell sat slumped in an easy chair surrounded by pale pink wool. A mass of gray yarn was twisted tightly around her throat.

"Looks like she did a lot of needlework," Uncle Rankin said. Of course he knew all about that, same as everyone else in town, but somebody had to say something. Mr. Byrd gulped and ran for the john. Afterwards he smoothed back his hair and perched on the edge of a flimsy little chair with bow legs while we traipsed around the room taking pictures and looking through Nell's sewing bag.

Even as she died, Nell must have been at work on another picture for Lettie: a bra stuffed with Kleenex, the empty box sitting next to the undergarment. The box was the old-fashioned one, dark blue and white instead of these flowery designer things nowadays. Easier to copy, I guess. Anyhow, it boded no good for Lettie.

My nose was about to jump off my face and, too late, it dawned on me that I didn't have hay fever. As for Uncle Rankin, he was making a real effort to get all the facts.

"She must have made a lot of enemies," he said.

Mr. Byrd shifted uneasily. I could tell he felt bound to defend Nell's honor but there wasn't any use. He shrugged and settled for the truth.

"My wife had a sharp tongue and a sharp needle, but she never based her gossip on a lie."

"Did she get money for her little—hobby?"

The old gentleman's face flushed. "Money? Goodness, no. She didn't want to keep secrets. That was part of her pleasure, I'm afraid, embarrassing people in front of their friends."

"Why didn't you put your foot down? Tell her to stop?"

Mr. Byrd gazed at him a minute. "Are you married, Chief?"

Uncle Rankin, one of the most married men I know, blushed and backed off a little. "But surely she'd have listened to reason. I mean, the legal problems. Libel and all that."

"I told you, my wife did not lie. No one ever sued. I guess they preferred to forget the whole thing."

"Someone didn't," I said.

An hour later I sat at a table in Jeeter's Place trying to mull over the whole business. I was sorry about Lettie because I always did like her spunk, but—my nose twitched—but what? What if it wasn't Lettie?

In most cases it pays to check out the spouse, but Mr. Byrd was clean. He might have tried to get free after ten years with Nell, but after forty? Why bother?

Sadie Miller was too saintly to get even with anybody. Clara Lou Stokes is a frail little thing—no match for Nell—but I figured Ed might be a possibility.

Jeeter brought me another Cherry Coke without being asked, shot me a lecherous glance and ambled away without a word. I think he was hoping I'd "break the case" in his establishment. Good for business.

Maybe Mr. Collins was the silencer. Not personally, of course. He had enough money to hire somebody to do it, but I'd have heard if there was a stranger in town. There wasn't.

So back to Lettie. I remembered the Kleenex box and my nose pitched a fit. That settled it. I had to go back to the house. The body would be gone, thank God. Crestview Funeral Home had hauled Nell away. There's no crest and no view but it's the only show in town. Mr. Byrd had gone with them so I scrounged up a skeleton key and walked over, letting myself in.

Not knowing what I was looking for, I climbed the stairs, rubbing my nose all the way. In the bedroom the old lady's presence was everywhere—flung across chairs, creeping out of drawers, hanging on the bedpost. By contrast, Mr. Byrd's bureau looked like an ad for one of those high-class furniture stores. Not a speck of dust. A comb, brush and hand mirror were lined up at a slant. A jar of hair conditioner and scented hairspray balanced each side. There was nothing else to see.

Without any warning the front door slammed and footsteps sounded on the stairs. I stepped into a closet and pulled the door almost shut, my nose still doing a number. Pinstripes closed in around me. Even in the dark I could see rows of spotless, dignified shoes. Felt like I was at a banker's convention.

Mr. Byrd walked into the room and knelt by the four poster. I didn't like spying on his grief but there wasn't much else to do. It gets boring real fast in a closet. I tried to move my head but had a choice of hugging my collar bone or chinning myself on the rod. I turned sideways and stuck my nose into a furry object that tickled like crazy.

Mr. Byrd stood up with something in his hand just as I blundered out of the closet with something in mine. His pink face reddened up. Those mild little eyes seemed to pop.

"Ah . . ." I began.

"No one else knew," he stammered.

"Choo," I finished, blowing him back a step.

"No one! She was going to show the whole world."

I took the needlepoint canvas he held. The mattress had pressed it flat as a road possum, but it was a good likeness, all right. Would've been a big hit at his birthday party. The half-finished portrait showed Mr. Byrd reading in bed, his gray sideburns mighty sparse next to the pink of his spreading scalp. And there I stood with his spare mop in my other hand.

I guess Nell thought she could make a bald statement and get away with it. She just didn't understand. If any man says vanity is a woman's vice, I bet you a Cherry Coke at Jeeter's he has himself a full head of healthy hair.

A Salutary Witness

Leila Davis

The hostess stopped Inspector Turner before he could head for his favorite lunch table. After a furtive glance over her shoulder, she leaned forward, keeping her voice low. "There's a rather odd woman sitting at your table. She insists she's having lunch with you."

"I wasn't expecting anyone." The table was out of Turner's view. "What's odd about her?"

"She's reading a dictionary."

"Damn! Sorry." Scowling, Turner stuffed his hands in his pockets. "If I try to slip out, she'll track me down somewhere else."

The hostess looked surprised. "You know her?"

"Afraid so. She's my mother." Shoulders squared, he headed for the table, determined to remain calm.

Mrs. Felicity Gaudett sat with her back to him, her white hair standing out like a beacon against the dark paneling of the walls. "Did you know that 'edentate' means having few or no teeth?" she asked, her attention still focused on the paperback dictionary before her.

"Hullo, Mum." Turner slid into the chair opposite her. "Did you have your mirror rigged so you could see me coming?"

"I didn't have to, I heard you. What kind of mother would I be if I couldn't recognize my own children's footsteps?" She pushed her slipping bifocals up on her nose, fixing her gaze on him.

Ignoring her rhetorical question, he drove the conversational ball back into her court. "I thought you were spending your summer holiday in Devon with Hayley."

"I am. The children send their thanks to Uncle Dan for the presents. I came up to London to see you on business."

Turner hoped against hope that she meant business connected with her investments, though she'd never once consulted him about them before. "Let's order lunch first, then you can tell me about it."

"I'll have the diet plate. You have to stop a murder."

"That is one of the things the Yard pays me to do, along with catching murderers." He shifted his attention to the waiter, now standing at the end of the table. "The chicken curry for me."

"The first two deaths were an accident, but the next one is cold, premeditated murder."

"Just this once, Mum, start at the beginning and tell me what happened in chronological order." Turner knew his mother's habit of going off on tangents and backtracking. "Let's have a straight-forward, bald-facts story."

"Mr. Penworthy—he lived in that big manor house we always pass on the way to Hayley's—and his daughter were killed five weeks ago when a drunk driver struck their car head-on. That's the accident I mentioned." Mrs. Gaudett paused to let that sink in. "Since then, the widow claims her young stepson Colin has had two accidents. She thinks someone is trying to kill the boy."

"Then Mrs. Penworthy should go to the local police."

"She has, and is not satisfied with the results. The first time, Colin was playing Tarzan, swinging from a rope tied to a large branch, and the rope broke. Someone cut it two-thirds of the way through." Whisking her dictionary off the table, Mrs. Gaudett leaned back to allow the waiter to set her plate before her. "Colin suffered several bruises but no broken bones."

Turner picked up his fork, ready to do justice to his curry. "I repeat, it's a matter for the local police."

"They made enquiries, then dropped it." The efficient way Mum polished off her salad told Turner she planned to bombard him with the main force of her argument when she'd finished and had no distractions. "Five days later, Colin fell down the staircase, suffering a mild concussion. When the police questioned him, he said he'd tripped over something that felt like a wire, but the police found no evidence of a wire. No scratches on the balusters, or anything like that."

"It's possible he imagined it. He may have thought he needed a more dramatic explanation than admitting he was clumsy." Turner fixed a serious gaze on his mother. "After all, this does make him the center of attention."

"I see." Mrs. Gaudett absently tapped her fingers on the edge of her empty plate. "That doesn't explain the cut rope."

"The boy could have done that, too. Think of it this way: His father and sister are dead; everyone talks about what a tragedy it was and how wonderful they were, and there sits Colin, feeling neglected. So he finds a way to put himself in the limelight. You mentioned he's Mrs. Penworthy's stepson?"

"Yes, the poor child lost his real mother a few years ago to cancer. Now his father and sister." A sad shake of her head expressed Mrs. Gaudett's feelings. "You don't think he's in any real danger?"

"Only from himself." Turner added milk to his coffee and stirred it. "If his stepmother's the hysterical sort, she'll be smothering him with attention. I don't suppose your new diet allows you to have a sweet? Yogurt with fruit?" It took an effort to keep a smile off his face when he saw her wrinkle her nose.

"You know what I think of yogurt! I'll have the double chocolate and cherry torte. The calories I saved by not putting sugar and milk in my tea balance out the torte, and I had a salad, so I'm still below my calorie allowance."

The glint in her eyes warned him not to contest her logic. In a matter of moments, Mum had her chocolate and Dan, out of pure devilishness, sat across from her virtuously eating yogurt and strawberries.

"You wouldn't consider recommending to the Devon police that they keep an eye on Colin?" asked Mrs. Gaudett, ignoring her son's blatant—albeit silent—reprimand.

The inspector took a deep breath. He should have seen that coming. "Mother, the Yard doesn't interfere with local matters, and if it did, I wouldn't be the one making a recommendation. No British police force has the resources to provide protection for private citizens in a situation like this. If Mrs. Penworthy is concerned about the lad, she should engage someone to protect him."

A disdainful sniff preluded Mrs. Gaudett's next remark. "I

think 'edentate' describes the police quite well—few or no teeth."

"We do the best we can. And *you* are not to interfere."

Offended, she tilted her chin at a haughty angle. "Daniel, your mother *never* interferes."

During the train ride back to Devon, Mrs. Gaudett decided the worried mother might welcome a second pair of eyes in watching over young Colin. A witness who could swear the boy was in real danger.

Two days later, Mrs. Gaudett sat in the small salon of Penworthy Hall, sipping plain tea and listening to the widow describe her stepson's narrow escapes. As she listened, Mrs. Gaudett carefully assessed her young hostess's honey-blonde hair, sleek figure, designer frock, and diamonds. Diamond earrings, diamonds in her wedding and engagement rings, and a large, square-cut diamond on her right hand. Even her watch had a border of diamonds around the face.

Did she put those on to dazzle me, wondered Mrs. Gaudett. They're the sort of things I'd expect to see at a London gala, not in a country home on a weekday.

"The police simply won't listen to me," complained Alicia Penworthy. "That Sergeant Gibbs keeps telling me nine-year-old boys are prone to accidents, and they eventually get over their awkwardness. I think he even suspects Colin of cutting that rope himself!" She ended on an indignant note, her breathing quick.

"I remember the scrapes my boys got into when they were growing up," Mrs. Gaudett sympathized. "I swear Dan had a bruise or a cut somewhere on his body from the time he started crawling until he turned eleven. But never anything like your poor lad has suffered."

"Oh, I admit Colin has his share of minor disasters. But I'm not an overprotective mother, nor am I so paranoid after the accident that took my husband and daughter, that I'm given to imagining things." She leaned slightly forward, her voice again indignant. "The police suggested Colin and I needed to get away for a nice, long holiday. But school starts in less than a fortnight, and I'm not going to disrupt Colin's life any further by having him miss his classes."

"Very sensible of you. May I ask you a personal question, Mrs. Penworthy? Is there anyone who would benefit from Colin's death? That might give the police a definite suspect."

Alicia glanced around her, as if making sure no one eavesdropped. She lowered her voice. "I don't want to make any accusations I can't prove, but my brother-in-law will inherit Penworthy Hall, and the land, if anything happens to Colin. Of course, Matthew's much too clever to do his dirty work himself. I think he's engaged one of the locals."

"Oh, dear, that is serious." Mrs. Gaudett raised her eyebrows slightly. "I don't mean to pry, but what would become of *you* then? To lose your entire family, then be turned out of your home, is too horrible to contemplate."

Alicia put on a brave smile. "Robert's insurance left me enough to get by on, at least until I find a situation. I was private secretary to one of Robert's London friends when we met. He'd probably give me a reference."

Mrs. Gaudett put down her cup and sat back, both hands firmly clenching her handbag to resist reaching for a second chocolate-iced biscuit. "You poor child. Having to go back to work, and in a place as noisy as London, after the peaceful life you've had here. That would be terribly distressing for you."

"If anything happened to Colin, I couldn't stay on here. In London, at least I'd be away from painful memories." Alicia stopped her trembling lips by compressing them.

"I know full well what it means to lose a loved one, having been widowed twice myself, though I still have my children to comfort me." Mrs. Gaudett let a sympathetic sigh escape. "Now, I don't pretend that I could protect Colin from a direct attack, but as a mother and grandmother, I'm sure I can keep a close eye on him. We'll have no more unexplained accidents."

Alicia beamed a smile at her. "I'm sure I can rely on you. You understand this is just until he returns to school. He should be safe there."

"Certainly. I agree the lad's danger will lessen then."

When introduced to Colin as his new nanny—his last one had been dismissed five years before—Mrs. Gaudett noticed that his reaction stopped just short of a sneer. The lad was bright enough to guess the real reason for her presence. He obviously didn't think a short, overweight woman, past the half-century mark, was much of a protector. Mrs. Gaudett gave him a brisk nod and a smile, satisfied to be accepted at face value.

"I'd appreciate it if you'd show me your room, Colin, then you can tell me about yourself."

Colin sulkily showed her his bedroom, his plastic dinosaur collection, and the miniature city he'd constructed out of Legos. Every attempt to discuss either with him elicited little more than a grunt in response.

His bookshelf contained *Ivanhoe, Robin Hood, Kidnapped, Treasure Island*, three Tarzan books, some comics, and assorted paperback adventures. Mrs. Gaudett looked them over, then wandered into the adjoining bathroom.

"Which medicines do you take?" she called.

Colin joined her in front of the open shelf. "I take two vitamins in the morning. The rest of the stuff is for when I'm unwell."

Mrs. Gaudett picked up a prescription medicine, then read the label. "I see you have problems with allergies. So have I. Miserable way to go through life, isn't it, always sneezing and wheezing and itching eyes. What are yours?"

"I haven't had problems for ever so long. It's mostly things I can't eat, and I know they'll make me sick, so I don't eat them."

"Very sensible of you." Mrs. Gaudett noticed he had three different strengths of medication for his allergy reactions. "My youngest son is allergic to grass. He could never mow the lawn, or be near an open window when someone else mowed it."

Their shared ailments, as well as Mrs. Gaudett's interest in *him*, overruled Colin's former surliness and loosened his tongue. "My friend at school, Barstow Minor, can't be around roses. The only time it really bothers him is Parents' Day, when we have part of the ceremonies in the rose garden. I've never passed out like he has, but I was rushed to hospital once when we were visiting at Gran's and I ate some shrimp salad." He sounded quite proud of the event.

"That must have been a frightening experience." Mrs. Gaudett put the bottles back on the shelf and switched out the light. "Your mother told me you have a very nice bicycle. I brought mine along, too. Suppose we ride into the village. We can each buy a new book, and I need more stamps."

If it surprised Colin that Mrs. Gaudett rode a ten-speed bike, or that she had little difficulty keeping up with him, he didn't say anything. Having her dog his steps in the village, however, roused querulous comment. "You don't have to follow me everywhere. Mum doesn't. I can meet you at the post office."

Mrs. Gaudett impaled him with the force of her gaze. "I've spent too many hours of my life searching for small boys. At my age, I no longer have that much time to waste. We'll stay together."

Though his stepmother had never spoken to him in that tone, Colin knew he'd met an implacable force. Muttering to himself, he conceded. On the return trip home, he tried outrunning her on his bicycle, chagrined when she stayed on his tail. When they reached Penworthy Hall, Mrs. Gaudett dismounted, smiling, and only slightly short of breath.

"I always enjoy a bit of brisk exercise. In my younger days, I won several awards as a racer." She chucked him under the chin. "An experienced rider always has sufficient sense to draft the lead rider."

The remainder of the week passed without incident. Sunday, Mrs. Gaudett joined her daughter's family for church and took lunch with them. Knowing the Penworthy cook would leave for her half day after lunch, Mrs. Gaudett planned to return to the Hall by one o'clock.

An ambulance in front of the entrance greeted her when she arrived back at Penworthy Hall. Heart pounding, Mrs. Gaudett rushed forward. Two men came down the steps, carrying Colin on a stretcher. Alicia Penworthy followed, sobbing and clenching her hands.

"What's happened?" demanded Mrs. Gaudett.

"He was playing with his remote control airplane on the terrace," said Alicia, sniffing. "Someone dug a hole under one of the flagstones, then covered it over with the stone. When Colin stepped on it, it gave way and he struck his head again."

Grimly, Mrs. Gaudett marched around the house to examine the hole, in the section of terrace closest to the hedge. This section was also out of direct view of the windows or door, unless someone looked out at an angle. Or the villain could have done his digging under cover of darkness. But what was the *reason* for the hole? A shallow one, at that.

Mrs. Gaudett knew the staff had the day off, so only Alicia had been home to keep an eye on her son. Everyone in the village probably knew the Sunday routine at the Hall. Even an outsider wouldn't have difficulty learning of it.

Collecting Colin's plane and controls, Mrs. Gaudett took them to his room. She was alone in the house; Alicia had gone with Colin in the ambulance. After several minutes of thought, Mrs. Gaudett's "motherly misgivings" prodded her to make a judicious investigation of some of the other rooms. She never considered it snooping, or an invasion of privacy, when she acted to protect others against their own poor judgment.

Anytime the children were too perfect, she mused, I always knew they were up to no good. And someone around here has definitely been too good to be real.

The doctor kept Colin in the hospital overnight for observation. After returning home, the lad had to stay quiet. Mrs. Gaudett read to him, told him stories about her children, and listened to him describe his accidents.

"The first one didn't really hurt me much, and I thought I'd have a jolly time telling my chums about it at school. But I'm tired of these falls. They give me the most awful headache."

"I can well imagine," said Mrs. Gaudett. "It took a broken leg to convince my Dan he should pay more heed to what he was doing. We can be grateful you haven't broken any bones."

Alicia hovered nearby, overly solicitous of her stepson. When Mrs. Gaudett asked Colin why he'd been playing on the terrace with his plane, rather than going out into the more open space of the lawn, Alicia answered for him. "I wanted Colin within my view. I was sitting on the chaise lounge, reading, and didn't see him fall. Thank God I was close enough to get to him straightaway."

"Yes, that was fortunate," Mrs. Gaudett agreed.

Friday, Colin rebelled against his confinement, but his stepmother still felt reluctant to let him outside. After arguing over it for fifteen minutes, Alicia suggested a picnic on the coast. While Colin dressed for it, Alicia confided in Mrs. Gaudett.

"All these 'accidents' have happened here. If we get away for the day, he should be safe. We haven't made any advance plans that anyone could know about."

"I'll change into something more suited to picnics, then," said Mrs. Gaudett. She reappeared shortly, clad in a bright yellow running suit and trainers. "When I go out into the country, I like to wear something bright enough to be seen, in case I lose my way. I don't want a search party to miss me."

Alicia and Colin, in jeans and blue sweatshirts, looked quite drab in comparison. Mrs. Gaudett volunteered to take the back seat, so the bright sunlight wouldn't bother her eyes. The picnic basket shared the seat with her.

When they reached their destination, Alicia grabbed the picnic hamper and set off for the high point of the cliffs, about a mile distant. Mrs. Gaudett pulled on a knapsack, with her handbag inside, and followed. Colin walked between the two women.

The view made the hike well worth the effort. A light wind ruffled the sea, and an adventurous sailboat skimmed across the surface. Gulls, hoping for a free lunch, circled the picnickers. Colin tossed them the crusts of his sandwiches.

Less than three minutes after finishing his last sandwich, Colin experienced difficulty breathing. Clutching at his throat, he turned panicked eyes toward his stepmother.

"My God, he's having an allergic reaction," shrieked Alicia. "We have to get him to hospital."

"We're a mile from the car," said Mrs. Gaudett. "He's incapable of walking that far, and we can't carry him fast enough. You run to the car and get help. The Coast Guard or someone can come for him with a helicopter."

Alicia grabbed the gasping boy, trying to pull him to his feet. "You don't understand. If he doesn't get help fast, he'll die."

"I *do* understand," said Mrs. Gaudett, prying the frantic woman free. "*Run.* Your son's life depends on it. Tell the helicopter to look for a bright yellow object."

Alicia hesitated a moment longer, then began running. Mrs. Gaudett seated herself, opened her knapsack, then her handbag. From it she extracted a small plastic bottle of water and Colin's strongest medication for allergic reaction. Propping his head up, she put a tablet on his tongue, then held the water to his mouth for him to drink.

"Calm down now, laddie. You're safe. Your panic aggravates the symptoms, you know. I've been through this dozens of times myself, and with my son, so I know exactly what to do. Let's think about how much fun it will be if they send a helicopter for us."

Reassured by her calm tone, Colin's wheezing slowed as he relaxed. Mrs. Gaudett cradled his head on her lap, stroking his hair. The lad was breathing easily by the time the helicopter arrived. Mrs. Gaudett had a whispered conversation with the doctor, then joined Colin in the excitement of their first helicopter ride. Alicia, the doctor explained, was already on the way to St. Bartholomew's in her car.

At the hospital, Alicia, near hysteria, rushed into Colin's room, screaming at the staff to save her son. When she saw Colin sitting on the bed, reading a comic, she abruptly stopped, then jerked her head around to face Mrs. Gaudett. Her expression showed confusion and bewilderment. "You saved him," she mumbled.

Mrs. Gaudett turned an accusing gaze on the younger woman. "Yes, I did. When I first saw Colin's allergy medication, I took the precaution of slipping a couple of the strongest tablets into my handbag. I intended to return them when I left your employ, if they weren't needed before then." Moving forward, she placed a firm hand on Alicia's arm. "There's someone in the corridor who wishes to speak to you."

Inspector Turner offered to take his mother to dinner at the restaurant of her choice *if* she'd refrain from saying "I told you so" while explaining how she concluded that Alicia was trying to murder Colin. She met him at Scotland Yard, then the pair took a leisurely stroll through St. James Park to "work up an appetite," as she said.

"Alicia hated being stuck down there in the country. Like all old family homes, Penworthy Hall is expensive to maintain, so she really didn't mind if her brother-in-law inherited it. After her husband died, she collected his insurance money, but he'd had none on his daughter. Not many families think it worth the expense to buy life insurance on their children. After the accident, her solicitor suggested that Alicia insure both herself and Colin. The policy had a double-indemnity clause."

"And that gave her the idea of killing him." Turner gazed down on the mother who'd so often promised him a short life while he was growing up. He was glad hers had been idle threats.

"Death duties took a substantial amount of Alicia's assets. Then she had the expense of keeping Colin in school. She could have stayed on there by living frugally, but Alicia longed for the social whirl she'd known in London before her marriage, where people admired and appreciated her beauty. You see, she was several years younger than her husband, and mistakenly thought he was quite wealthy."

"And disillusionment didn't endear him to her."

They were interrupted by a pair of Japanese tourists asking directions to Buckingham Palace. Turner had to repeat himself three times before he could make himself understood.

"So near and yet so far," murmured Mrs. Gaudett. "Getting back to Alicia, Mr. Penworthy married her mainly to provide a mother for his children, which added to her resentment. With the insurance she planned to receive after Colin's death, she hoped to capture a richer prize while she still had her beauty."

"You gleaned all this from the servants?"

Mrs. Gaudett smiled and waved at someone across the park. Her stalling tactic failed to deceive her son. "I don't gossip with servants, Daniel. I simply put my motherly misgivings and knowledge of human nature to the test."

"Ah. You snooped."

That earned a disdainful sniff from Mum. "I *observed.* You said Colin could be staging those accidents to make himself the center of attention. It occurred to me that Alicia could be using them as camouflage for a real murder. If one of the accidents *did* kill the child, fine. She cut through the rope, and she sabotaged the flagstone. The hole was too shallow to be intended to do much harm."

"What about the stairs? Did Alicia push the lad?"

"No. Colin said he tripped on the third step. I examined the baluster carefully and found no scratches. But Alicia could have wrapped something around a wire to cushion it. The stairs are carpeted, and the pile thick enough that a tack, or some other small object, would never be seen. Then she could have removed it before she called for help."

Turner nodded. "I suppose that explanation is as good as any."

Mrs. Gaudett stepped off the path to let a nanny pushing a pram pass them. "My suspicions regarding Alicia were confirmed when I happened to notice a tin of shrimp in the top drawer of her dressing table. Before the picnic, she ground up some shrimp and mixed it in with the fish paste in Colin's sandwiches. She knew we'd never have time to get him to hospital before he died from the reaction. And there I was, the senile old lady, still sane enough to be a salutary witness to her frantic efforts to save her stepson."

Chuckling, Turner tucked his mother's arm through his. "That's what happens when employers don't ask for references. I could have told her you aren't senile. Unscrupulous, sly, suspicious, snoopy, single-minded, smug, but never senile."

"That's no way to speak of your mother, Daniel. As for Alicia, she has a facinorous personality." Mrs. Gaudett glanced sideways, smiled at her son's clenched jaw, then continued. "Wouldn't you call a woman who tried to murder a child exceedingly wicked?"

"I would. I can pronounce wicked!"

If Wishes Could Kill

Linda Weiser Friedman

"No, Lev. I haven't seen her today." Chaya Dirotte stood in her kitchen, one large hip resting awkwardly against a cutlery drawer, the telephone receiver sandwiched between her left shoulder and her ear. She got a flame going under the large teakettle.

Lev Steinhammer was looking for his wife. "Mrs. Dirotte."

Chaya rolled her eyes. She had long ago given up trying to get her friend's husband to call her by her first name. Oh, well. Maybe when she completed her Ph.D. Surely, he'd rather call her Chaya than *Doctor* Dirotte. Chaya ripped a piece of notepaper off the thick pad that always lay next to her toaster.

I should move that notepad somewhere else, she thought. It *was* a fire hazard. But she didn't move it. Instead she waddled over to the breakfast bar that separated the small dining room from the even smaller kitchen. The phone was still perched next to her ear, and the gritty voice of her friend's husband still insisted that she come clean about his wife's present whereabouts, and she still repeated one way or another that she hadn't been consulted before her friend decided to move out on the gritty voice.

Chaya often noticed things like fire hazards, but seldom did anything about them. Besides, she liked her notepaper right where it was, near the phone. The voice in her ear was growing more agitated. Maybe she should move the toaster. Chaya maneuvered herself onto a tall stool, wincing as her seven-month belly with its turned out button grazed the rim of the breakfast counter. She sat sideways, her belly making what appeared to be an extension of the counter top.

"Lev," she said finally, "I don't have time for this." But she continued to listen to him anyway. At the top of the small sheet of paper she wrote, in capital letters, TO DO. She had already made up a to-do list for today, but she couldn't find it. A lot of good it did her. She looked at her watch. 11:40. She had to be at the school at exactly 12:15 to pick up her daughter Sharon from nursery school. She said a mental prayer, hoping that the two pairs of extra thick training panties would still be dry today when she got the little one home.

She clicked the ball-point pen, nervously, in and out. In and out. She wrote, *Give the kids a bath*, and underlined it. Beneath it she wrote, *Buy olive oil and wicks for the menorah.* Then she smiled to herself. Since starting graduate school, she hadn't exactly been the model *balabusta*, the perfect housewife and mother, that she had always imagined she would be. Invariably, *Give the kids a bath* was the top entry in her to-do list and, just as invariably, the list itself, along with this and other terribly important notations, was nowhere to be found by the time Zahava came home from school at half past three.

Suddenly, the voice at the other end of the phone grew softer and Chaya, not even realizing what she was doing, felt her back tense up and her fingers tighten their grip around the pen and her free hand reach up to settle the receiver more carefully against her ear.

"I mean it, Mrs. Dirotte. I will do it. I really will."

Do what? She had missed it. Something to do with Yankel, the Steinhammers' four-year-old boy.

"I know he's in school today. I just talked to his teacher."

"Of course he's in school today, Lev. He's in school every day." What had she missed? Was it some sort of threat?

"Well, you just tell my wife . . ."

"*If* I see her . . ."

". . . *if* you see her . . . tell her that, just tell her."

This was her chance. "What exactly should I tell Rina if I see her?"

"Tell her if she doesn't come back where she belongs and do her job as a loving, religious wife and mother, I can't be responsible for what happens."

"For what happens to whom?"

"You just tell her. She'll know what I'm talking about."

Chaya stared at the dead phone in her hand and then consulted her watch. 11:55. She knew where Yankel went to school. Rina and Lev still hadn't decided on a yeshiva for him, and her girls' yeshiva accepted some boys into their preschool classes. It was back in March that she had convinced her friend to send him there for the time being. Which was a big help, considering Rina had been very pregnant with twins at the time.

She pressed the big, flat button on the phone a couple of times, hard, and wriggled uncomfortably on the high stool. She'd have to make this fast and then run to the bathroom. Come the eighth month and she was forever running to pee. No matter what.

At the dial tone, Chaya keyed in the number of the school office. A young voice answered.

"Give me Mrs. Winter," she said crisply. "This is Chaya Dirotte." Shula Winter, another school mother, had served with her on several PTA committees, and the two had grown quite close, mostly over the phone. Shula volunteered at the school office two mornings a week.

"Listen," Chaya said quickly, when she heard Shula's voice, "just say yes or no. Is anyone on any of the extensions?" Chaya knew that the various tiny cubicles were readily visible through glass partitions that shut out sound only, and not much of that.

"No."

"Okay. Do not—repeat—*do not*—allow anyone to pick up Yankel Steinhammer from school today."

"But, what . . . ?"

"This is important, Shula. I can't explain right now and I don't want anyone to know. Find the boy. Get his coat. Bring him to the office and keep him with you. *With you.*" Chaya took a deep breath and heaved her bulk off the stool. She held on tightly to the edge of the tabletop. "Understand?"

"I think so."

"I will get him from you when I pick up my Sharon. Okay?"

"Yes."

"If anyone asks, you don't know anything about anything."

"That's certainly true."

"I owe you one."

"That's true, too."

She checked her watch again. Just enough time to check in with the small office she'd made for herself at the top of the stairs. She carried a steaming mug of decaf in one hand and a tuna-wheat sandwich in the other. Past the dining room and up the stairs, trying hard not to look at the once-formal dining room table, now strewn with her open books and scholarly magazines and photocopied articles and the spiral notebooks partially filled with the chicken scratchings she called notes. Ph.D., indeed. She sighed, urging her thick body to move a little faster. And, anyway, what's a nice, *frum*, Jewish woman—a *mother*, no less—doing, going for a degree in Religious Philosophy? Oh, well.

She opened the door slowly and quietly and edged her way into the cramped study. The old porta-crib blocked half the book shelves; a stack of paper diaper boxes blocked the other half. Natural winter sunlight filtered thinly through ancient slatted blinds.

There was the overstuffed rocking chair in which she had nursed first Zahava, then Sharon. Soon another one. Another hungry mouth, another bundle of need.

Chaya stood quietly for a moment watching the comfortable rocker creak forward and back, an inch at a time.

Rina, head thrown back, jaw slack, stared at the ceiling, or at nothing. The twins, one infant in each arm, suckled noisily at her breasts. Somehow—Chaya couldn't figure out exactly how—each baby managed to keep a generous nipple in his own greedy little mouth. One, the one on Rina's right, paused for a moment for a quick breath, and white, creamy milk ran down his cheek. Then he resumed, as noisily as before.

Rina's breasts were full, nature had seen to that. They stood out in awkward contrast to the rest of her pale, bony form. The paler skin of the short white line that ran down her left breast was, Chaya knew, a remnant of the time that Rina had gotten in the way of a steak knife. The bruise on her left cheek was first coming out now in showy colors of blue and purple and green. The skin around her right eye, blackened for a week, was beginning to fade to a pale yellow. One day, maybe Rina would cap those two front teeth. Chipped as they were, she looked like a refugee from a mental ward. Or a bag lady. Or something. Chaya shook her head. Orthodox Jews just didn't *do* that to their wives. At least, that's what she'd always thought.

Either Rina hadn't heard her come in, or she didn't care. She hadn't cared about much lately. It had been all Chaya could do to convince her—finally—to leave her husband. Even coming here today took more willpower than Rina could have mustered alone.

Chaya put the food down on the desk at Rina's side. "I have to go now, Rina," she whispered. "To pick up Sharon at school."

Rina looked at her with large, brown eyes that were red from lack of sleep.

Impulsively, Chaya bent over and kissed her friend on the forehead.

"I've been good to him, haven't I, Chay?" Rina whispered back.

"Yes, you've been very good to him." The bastard. "Now, just relax until I get back with the kids." Chaya bit her tongue. If Rina caught the plural form of the word she didn't react. Chaya turned to go.

"You know," Rina continued, "I even left him supper." Chaya looked back sadly. Supper? For that *momzer*? Rina was still talking, her eyes closed now. "Spicy beef stew . . . lots of *schmaltz* . . . his favorite . . . I left it on the stove, just for him." Could this be the same girl who had kicked up such trouble during their high school years? "With a special surprise." Then she smiled, almost.

Well, Chaya thought, if I have *my* way, that's the last meal you'll ever prepare for him.

They came for her in a big car. In the middle of the night, like the thieves that they were. The women were of early middle age and the car, of a matching vintage, was large and black and had mud smeared over its license plates.

The Orthodox Jewish Women's Shelter guarded its secret location very carefully and even Rina herself didn't know where the two helpful, energetic women were taking her. Somewhere on Long Island, and when Rina found herself there she wouldn't tell anyone, not even Chaya.

Chaya helped Rina bundle the babies into their snow-white bunting. When they were swaddled securely, they seemed to be three times their actual size, their tiny, round faces peering out in confusion at the great bustle of activity all around them. The two women from the shelter loaded Rina's things into the car. Two suitcases, one duffel bag, many boxes of paper diapers. The small

Chanukah menorah, a present from Chaya's husband, Shalom, with which Rina would usher in the upcoming festive holiday. "It's a time of miracles," he had told her. The car had even been prepared with two infant car seats in the back, into which they proceeded to strap the twins and next to which there was just enough room for Yankel to settle in, an old ragged stuffed bear in one hand while the other, rolled into a tight little fist, was slowly rubbing a sleepy eye.

Chaya took her friend aside and gave her a big hug. "It'll be all right, Rina. They'll take good care of you."

"I know." Rina hugged her back. "I just . . ."

"What?"

"I wish I didn't have to go away."

"You can't let Lev hurt you anymore, Rina. You know that. And, besides, now he's threatened Yankel."

Rina nodded, her eyes empty. "It's just that . . . running away like this . . . in the dark . . ." She turned away and, with the back of her hand, quickly brushed a tear from the side of her face. Then she winced. It was the side with the fresh bruise. "I . . ." She took a breath. "I just wish that I could stay home and that he would go away. But," she cut Chaya off, "I know, I know, Chayke. He would never agree to that. Not right now, anyway. Sometimes, Chay, I wish he would just up and die, you know?"

Chaya nodded and kissed her friend on the cheek, wondering what it meant to wish your husband dead. To really wish, not just play at it.

Rina got in the back and took Yankel on her lap, where he promptly curled up into a large ball, his head resting against his mother's chest, his thumb moving ever so slightly in his mouth, his teddy bear hugged tight. Chaya shut the door and the car sped safely away.

Chaya woke up with a start. It didn't take much to awaken her these days. A movement from the unformed creature inside her. A sharp cry from Sharon, asleep in the room next door, in response to the ogres that populated her sleeping and waking. Being three years old was probably the ultimate acid trip.

Right now, although the baby was pounding energetically against her abdomen from the inside, and although Sharon was whimpering and Shalom was putting one arm through his robe the

43

wrong way, it was the heavy, insistent pounding on the front door that woke her up. She lifted her left arm to peer at the wristwatch that, since Sharon was born, had never left her, except during the rare, stolen moment of bodily hygiene. Almost six o'clock. She'd had four hours of sleep. Not bad.

Chaya threw a large housecoat over her nightgown and lumbered down the stairs in her bare feet. Shalom was already talking to Lev Steinhammer at the door as cold morning air wafted into the house. Chaya drew her housecoat more securely around her large body."

"Where is she? Where did she take them?" He was breathing quite heavily and it gave his voice a rasping quality and his words were slurred and indistinct. They came out "Where'dshetaethem?" Had he been drinking?

Shalom had an arm around him and was making little reassuring sounds. But Lev suddenly bent over at a sharp angle, clutching his abdomen.

"Damn thish vug."

Oh. Bug. He was obviously ill. Shalom kicked the door shut with his foot and helped Steinhammer over to the couch.

Chaya decided to stay where she was. All she needed now was to bring some strange virus to her children. Steinhammer's face seemed very pale, especially now, framed as it was against the soft red brocade of her favorite couch. Please don't let him be sick just now. The wiry strands of his dark brown beard stood out in contrast to the pasty white of his face. His breathing was heavy and labored and he was obviously in pain.

"Can I get you something, Lev?" asked Chaya.

He tilted his head back to look up at her, but he had trouble focusing. Even with all the pain he must have been in, his eyelids hung down in a sleepy droop and his jaw hung slack. "Rina," he rasped, "Mae me shupper."

"I know she did, Lev."

It was really strange the way his eyelids continued to droop. He settled back awkwardly against the soft upholstery, the crown of his head, covered by its large black *yarmulke*, barely touching the wall. "My fayorite." He gasped, and his next words came out in a croupy bark. "Where'sh Rina?"

Then, in the brief moment it took for her to prepare a response, his body jerked twice in a kind of double spasm and crumbled heavily toward the floor. All she heard for a brief second was a kind of sucking noise and then she didn't hear it anymore.

Chaya stood where she was for a split second. Petrified. Then she looked at Shalom. Who was looking back at her.

Then Zahava was calling from the top of the stairs, "Is everything all right, Mommy?" And then Shalom was rushing over to where Lev Steinhammer was lying on the floor, his body grotesquely twisted, shaking him and slapping his face, for what reason Chaya couldn't fathom, and asking him repeatedly if he was okay. A gob of what looked like vomit shot from his mouth in a sticky mass of orange and brown.

And then Chaya was running to the kitchen phone to summon the paramedics.

The next few days were a mire of confusion and raw emotion.

Chaya's books and papers and notes, hastily cleared off the dining room table in preparation for the Sabbath, were stacked on the rocking chair in her little office at the top of the stairs, and there they remained even through the festive days of Chanukah.

The weather turned wet and gray and cold and slushy. Zahava and Sharon wore every stitch of woolen and rubber and plastic outerwear ever devised for small children and Chaya was forever either putting them on or taking them off.

And, beginning with the paramedics, the heavy winter boots of city officials trampled and idled and stood in place and shifted back and forth from one foot to the other at the doorway, around the living room, through the dining room, into the kitchen, and along the first few steps leading to the second level.

Lev Steinhammer was dead. Ironic, in a way, since just a few hours before he collapsed in front of the red brocade couch, Chaya had silently pronounced the amen to Rina's fervent wish that her husband of six years would "just up and die." Now that wish had come dreadfully and horribly true. There was nothing malicious about it, though, unless a bacterium can be said to possess intent to kill.

Food poisoning. The paramedics had said it first. The same facial paralysis that Chaya and Shalom had noticed had affected the victim's—imagine! Lev Steinhammer a victim!—swallowing reflex. It was probably a severe kind of botulism reaction, they said. The victim had vomited up the contents of his stomach and then sucked most of it back in again through his windpipe. In layman's terms, he choked on his own vomit.

Shalom was lighting six candles in the menorah for the sixth night of Chanukah, and the children were hopping around—actually, Sharon probably had to use the potty again—singing the *Maoz Tsur*. Chaya was casting one aching, wistful eye at the door to her study at the top of the stairs, behind which lay her hopes of ever being called Doctor and earning a decent salary, and another eye towards the kitchen in which, she knew, stood a large bowl of potato pancake batter turning pink and brown. That's when the doorbell rang. Twice.

She recognized him at once. "Detective Macdonald," she said graciously, without feeling at all gracious about it. "Please come in."

His gray eyes looked out at her from under long black eyelashes, wet with snow. His nose was red and he needed a shave. Huddled as he was inside his thick gray parka, he appeared to be shivering slightly. He probably was. The air coming through the open door wafted right through the weave of her maternity pullover, leaving colonies of goosebumps in its wake.

"You sure, Mrs. Dirotte?" He shifted slightly in the doorway. "I know it's the dinner hour, and all . . ."

"Please come in, Detective. It's no bother. Really." This time she meant it. If only to finally get the door closed again.

He came in, shaking snowflakes off his parka and the parka off his husky frame. Well, maybe not husky, exactly. Certainly large, though. He caught her examining him and cracked an easy grin. "Six-three."

"Oh. Sorry." She felt her cheeks grow hot. "I don't get to see too many really tall people."

"It's okay. There aren't that many of us around."

"Well . . ." She pointed in the direction of the living room. "I guess you can see that I already cleaned up the . . . uh . . . crime scene.

"Oh," he waved a hand, "I'm not here about that. The forensics are all finished."

"Was the autopsy done yet?"

"Yeah." Now *he* was staring at *her*.

"Well?" she prodded. "Was it food poisoning?"

"Uh-huh. Myasthenia gravis, due to botulism."

So it *was* botulism. She shook her head and sighed. "What a shame." She couldn't remember ever knowing anyone who had had it. Much less died of it. "Where does someone get botulism nowadays?"

"Oh, that was easy."

Suddenly, Chaya knew where the botulism had come from, and why Detective Macdonald was there. And she wondered why she hadn't thought of it sooner. From the corner of her field of vision, she saw that Shalom and the girls had finished bringing in the sixth day of Chanukah and they were now heading over to where she stood with the detective, Sharon still hopping slightly from one foot to the other.

"He got it from the pot that was on the stove. It was full of clostridium botulinum. Did your friend say anything to you about what was in that pot, Mrs. Dirotte?"

She grabbed Sharon and ran with her to the potty in the bathroom.

"He thinks she did it, you know."

"Mmm." They were in her bed, as close as the three of them could ever get. Namely: Shalom, Chaya, and Chaya's belly. They snuggled close, her back to his front, each molding to the other's contours, all the way down, from torso to toes. Shalom nuzzled at her ear.

"Well?"

Chaya tilted her head to one side and Shalom kissed her earlobe, then sent a trail of tiny kisses sliding down her neck. His thick, curly beard tickled her, as always. Chaya giggled softly and wriggled with contentment. "Well what?"

Shalom had his arms around her and she clasped his hands in both of her own. Now she brought his hands up to her mouth and kissed them in turn, gently.

"She's your friend, what do you think?"

"You mean, do I think she intentionally gave him food poisoning? To kill him? Come on."

"She certainly," he said between kisses, "had enough of a reason." He used his teeth to pull her nightgown off one shoulder, then went back to kissing her as if he intended to cover every inch of skin, which he did.

"That she had," Chaya whispered. She felt the baby move and put his hands under her nightgown over the little elbow or knee or toe that was sticking up, making a hard little point in her abdomen. He kept his hands on the spot until long after the limb returned to some secret interior space.

"I don't know, Shalom. That seems too farfetched. I mean—" He unbuttoned her nightgown. "She—well, you saw what she was like." He gently slipped the nightgown up over her body, past the large belly with its hidden pointy creature, across the swollen breasts, kissing her face when it became visible as she used to do when undressing Zahava for bed, as she still did with Sharon. "She barely had the strength of will to feed the babies; it was all I could do to get her to save herself. Kill him?" She lifted her arms to help him and he bunched up the nightgown and tossed it over onto his bed. "I don't think so. How would she do it? She'd have to know that something contained that botulism bacterium and put it in the stew. I don't think so."

Now, she was on her back and he was straddling her swollen body, kissing madly the white, stretched skin. He followed with soft, silent kisses the course of a fine, pale blue vein from the top of her breast to the dark pink areola and licked an erect nipple, causing it to stand even firmer. "Anyway," she continued, her breath coming more quickly, "Detective Macdonald said that it wasn't just the botulism that did him in. He was obviously allergic to something he'd eaten and it aggravated the gastric upset." Slowly, Shalom made his way over the arc of her belly and around her stretched-out belly button.

It was his favorite, Rina had said.

Then, he wasn't kissing her anymore.

"Sorry to bother you again, Mrs. Dirotte." At ten o'clock the following morning, Detective Macdonald sat at the breakfast bar in the kitchen, his long fingers wrapped around a steaming mug of hot, black coffee. Chaya sat sideways, one elbow resting heavily on the countertop, sipping her peppermint tea.

"Please." She took a sip. "Call me Chaya. Everyone does." She didn't bother to tell him how much she hated the 'Mrs.' Most men, she'd discovered, simply didn't understand.

"Okay, Chaya." It came out 'Kaya.' "You call me Parker."

"Parker? Is that your first name?"

"Uh-huh. It was my mother's maiden name. Chaya," he began. Kaya again.

"Not Kaya," she corrected him. "Chaya. Like this. Chh—Chh—." She made the guttural sound of the Hebrew letter *chet*. "It's the sound you make when you clear your throat."

He tried clearing his throat. "Chh—Chhaya. How's that?" He laughed. "You probably think I'm from the sticks."

"Are you?"

He brought the mug up to his mouth and took a healthy swallow. "I guess so. Very small town in southern New Jersey. Ninety-nine percent Catholic; one percent contrary."

Chaya smiled. Those were probably the town Jews, she thought wryly.

Now, his expression turned serious. "Chaya," he said, "do you know why I'm here today?"

She stared into her teacup. "You want to know if I can tell you what foods Lev Steinhammer was allergic to."

He shook his head and took another swallow. "We already know what was in the pot, and that's what killed Mr. Steinhammer. What I came to ask you is if Mrs. Steinhammer said anything to you to indicate that she *intended*," he stressed the word, "to kill her husband. After all, until we find her, we can't ask her directly and the DA says we can't proceed without some evidence of intent."

"I really don't know where she is, Parker. As I told you, it's a very well-kept secret."

"How do you get in touch with her?"

Chaya shrugged. "I can't. But I gave you the number of the rabbi who helped her contact the shelter. And, anyway," she said, "what was in the pot?"

He didn't hear her. He was busy. He extended one finger of his right hand. "We've got motive. You see," he explained, "cops were called in twice in the past year to settle what we call a domestic dispute. Each time she was clearly beaten up pretty badly, but she refused to press charges. And the neighbors and friends we interviewed," now his soft gray eyes seemed almost translucent as they looked down into her own, "including you, Chaya, did not paint a pretty picture of the Steinhammers' home life." Chaya bit her lip and quickly took a sip of tea. Had she inadvertently helped to seal her friend's indictment for murder?

"You did the right thing," he said in a softer voice, "sending her away.

"Anyhow," he continued briskly, "so much for motive." He held up a second finger. "Opportunity. No problem. She cooked his meals. She cooked *that* meal. That goes for weapon, too." He raised a third finger.

"Was the botulism definitely from the pot on the stove?"

He nodded. "Definitely. A little deliberate undercooking, combined with the knowledge that he was allergic to the food . . . Some research at the local library would have been all she needed."

Chaya shivered. "Do you really think Rina killed her husband with her cooking?"

"You'd be surprised at the crazy ways spouses can think of to kill each other."

"And that's enough to build a murder case on?"

"Why, I thought I explained that, Chaya. That's why I'm here."

She looked up. There was something in his voice, something she couldn't place.

"Did Mrs. Steinhammer give you any indication—anything at all—that she intended to harm her husband with that stew she concocted?"

His favorite . . . I left it on the stove, just for him . . . With a special surprise . . .

"You see," he went on, just as if he hadn't noticed the look of utter astonishment on Chaya's face, "even though this fellow may have abused his wife, even if, shall we say, he may have deserved to die, if we determine that in addition to," he ticked off on three fingers again, "motive"— One. "—opportunity—" Two. "—weapon—" Three. "—we have," another finger went up, "*intent*, well, you can see how that would change this whole thing from an accident to premeditated murder."

Chaya stared into her cup, as if reading the remains would tell her what to say in response. A few small pieces of peppermint leaves floated inside.

His favorite . . . With a special surprise . . .

"So otherwise," he said carefully, "I guess we'll just have to close the case." He paused. "Are you sure she didn't say anything to you about her plans?"

Chaya hesitated. She remembered clearly Rina's comments

about the stew.

I wish he would just up and die. At the time, Chaya had thought it was simply wishful thinking, a Chanukah prayer of sorts. She opened her mouth to speak.

"Because," Parker Macdonald rushed on, "if she did tell you something—something incriminating, say, enough to start building a case on—we could charge her with her husband's murder . . ."

She quickly closed her mouth and looked at him. He didn't seem to notice her.

". . . bring her back here, put her children in foster care. You know, until the outcome of the trial." He took a breath. "And bail—well, I don't know, the judge may not consider her a good risk, you never know about these things. So—" suddenly he was looking directly at her, "what do you say?"

"Say? About what?"

"Did Mrs. Steinhammer," he pronounced each word carefully and distinctly, "indicate to you that she had deliberately undercooked the sausage in the stew?" His pale gray eyes continued to look directly into hers. Locked onto hers.

. . . on the stove, just for him . . .

I understand, she screamed loudly, inside her head. "No," she said aloud. But there was something wrong. It was all wrong.

"Thank you, ma'am." Macdonald stood up, his relief immediately obvious. "I'll be going now."

What was it? "Wait a minute, Parker."

He turned back to her and half sat down again on the high stool, keeping one long leg on the floor. His coffee was finished.

"Did you say sausage?"

He nodded. "It has a very high risk for botulism. Everyone knows that—"

"*Pork* sausage?"

"—you have to cook it very well. Kill the bacteria." He looked at her. "Of course, pork sausage."

Chaya stared at him. "Does that mean he was allergic to pork?"

"Sure. The medical examiner says lots of people are allergic to pork."

This wasn't happening. Chaya looked at her watch. It was getting closer to the time to pick Sharon up from school. Chaya slid off the stool and put a hand out to steady herself. "Parker," she said, "Jews don't eat pork. It's *treif.* Not kosher." She began to pace slowly across the small kitchen.

The detective raised his eyebrows. "That's not so, Chaya. I had a partner on the force. Eddy Goldstein. He was Jewish. Ate pork all the time."

Chaya took another circuit around the kitchen. She stopped at the large double sink. Leaned her back against it for support. "Wait a minute." She shook her head. "I still don't understand exactly what happened. What exactly," she asked Macdonald, "was in the pot on the stove?"

He took a small wire-bound notepad from his shirt pocket, flipped it open, found the page he wanted. "It was a kind of a stew," he said. "Very unusual. Spicy and fatty." He looked at her. "You won't like this but it's easy to hide the taste of anything you put into a dish like that."

"Just go on."

"Small pieces of beef," he read. "Carrots, spinach, potatoes, turnip, leek, onion, garlic, some other assorted vegetables. And plenty of pork sausage, removed from its casing." He flipped to another page of the little book. "We found the casing in the garbage."

"It just doesn't make sense." She had her eyes closed, hands covering her face.

"Do you want to sit down, Chaya?"

She ignored him. "It doesn't make sense," she repeated. "There are too many questions." She looked at him. "Lev Steinhammer was a despicable husband, but I would be surprised if he ever ate pork in his life."

"He did this time."

She shook her head. "You said he was allergic to it. You can't have a serious allergic reaction the first time you are exposed to an allergen. You are saying he had to have eaten pork before. But he was an Orthodox Jew. He went to synagogue every day. He didn't eat *treif.*"

"Do Orthodox Jews generally beat up their wives?"

She winced.

"Sorry."

"Anyway," she continued, "Rina certainly doesn't eat pork. And if you're saying that she bought it just to kill her husband, first of all," Chaya said with a conviction she did not feel, "she wouldn't kill anyone; she's just not a murderer. Second, where would she even *get* the stuff? Third, how would she know it would poison him? I mean, not *every* batch of pork has botulism, does it? No one could sell it if that were so."

"It's not the pork. Pork sausage. Most people know you have to cook sausage at high temperature to destroy the bacteria."

"That's just what I mean," she exploded. "Rina doesn't even know that much! She would have to have deliberately undercooked it. Where would she even have the *hava mina* to . . ."

"The what?"

"How would she know to do all that? To find the pork sausage—the right kind, the kind that grows botulism—to undercook it enough so that the bacteria can thrive, to know that her husband was allergic to a substance he should never have tasted. I don't know, Detective. There's something very wrong here. Something doesn't fit."

Macdonald stood up again. He closed his notepad and put it away, found his parka and slipped into it. "Sorry, Chaya, it doesn't look that strange to me. Anyhow, like I said, we have nothing to go on. So . . ." He shrugged.

Chaya nodded.

"You ever call your friend, why don't you ask her what was in that pot?"

"No—uh—I told you—"

He waved a hand. "I know, I know, you don't know where she is."

"Are you going to . . ." She let it hang.

"No reason," he shrugged again, "to disturb her while she's recuperating. You want a lift somewhere? To pick up your little girl?"

She had a fleeting mental picture of herself arriving at the small religious school in a police car driven by a large, rough-skinned, undercover police officer—an obvious *goy*. She smiled and shook her head.

Macdonald extended a hand and, after a slight hesitation, she took it. His handshake was warm and firm.

The door closed shut behind him just as she finished pressing the buttons of the special phone number Rina had given her. The rings vibrated softly in the instrument pressed to her ear. One, two. She was supposed to let it ring a long time. Tomorrow, she thought,

I really must get back to work on that thesis. Three. If my brain hasn't totally atrophied by now. She peeled the top sheet off her memo pad and began making a list. Four, five. *TO DO AFTER* she wrote at the top. Six. *Give kids a bath.* She underlined it twice. Seven rings. How much was a long time? *Start a diet. Do the sewing pile.* She wondered if anyone else had given Rina word about her husband. Well, there'd be time enough for that. *Get legs waxed.* She tapped her pencil lightly on the kitchen counter, then crossed out *Start a diet,* and added *Eat plenty of fruits and vegetables.*

It took eleven rings.

And then another ten minutes just to get Rina to the phone.

"Chaya! It's great to hear your voice."

Rina sounded better than she had in three years. She sounded—alive. "How've you been, Rina?"

"Great! Much better now that I don't have to worry about Lev anymore. They're very good to me here."

. . . I even left him supper . . .

"Rina." Chaya took a breath. "Do you remember you mentioned to me that you prepared Lev's favorite supper the day you left?" She hoped the police hadn't tapped her line.

A bitter voice echoed metallically in her ear. "Did he eat it?"

Chaya went cold.

. . . Spicy beef stew . . . Lots of schmaltz . . .

"Yes, Rina, he ate it," she whispered. What have you done?

. . . His favorite . . .

"Good!" There was that laugh again. "I sure taught him a lesson!" Then, her friend's voice was lower, more confidential in tone. "Do you know what I put in it, Chay?"

. . . Just for him . . . Wth a special surprise . . . I wish he would
. . . Yes. "What Rina?"

. . . just up and die . . .

"Pork!" Muted, yet triumphant, the voice she thought she knew as well as any other continued, "That big hypocrite! Wait 'til I tell him he ate a whole plateful of *treifus.* And licked his lips too, I'll bet."

Chaya felt faint. She'd been holding her breath without realizing it. She let it out now and automatically glanced at her wristwatch: 11:55. Time to go pick up Sharon.

"Did he say if he liked it?"

Glossary

balabusta—accomplished homemaker
frum—religious
goy—gentile
hava mina—presumption
Maoz Tsur—Hebrew song, celebrating the holiday of Chanukah, traditionally sung after lighting the menorah
menorah—the nine-branched Chanukah candelabrum
momzer—bastard
schmaltz—fat
treif—unfit for consumption according to Jewish law; not kosher
yarmulke—skullcap

The Dying Breed

Sally Miller Gearhart

Just off the northeast corner of the Maybrook Convalescent Home a brave mimosa tree determined to look beautiful and restful. Companion mimosas that had failed to look beautiful and restful had met the ax. "Survivor," Angela had labelled this one. From her ground-floor window she could touch a lower branch. If her window were open, that is. If they ever let up on that air conditioning so you could open a window around here, she thought.

Angela worried a fragment of corn from her upper left bicuspids and positioned it between her incisors for more focused mastication. From where she sat between her bed and the window she could view an acre of pavement, a sparsely populated parking lot blistering in the Memphis sun. The Administrator's maroon Accord inhabited the only bit of shade, compliments of the mimosa. That at least ought to protect the tree for a while, she mused. At least until this Administrator walked out or got replaced.

Behind her, Rose Santolla coughed. Angela knew without looking that Rose was reaching for the inhaler that fronted the ranks of medicine bottles and boxes on the far bedside table. She waited for the other two coughs, one short, one long, and then the inevitable wheeze before Rose's fist captured the inhaler. The plastic apple-green glass holding two-day-old zinnias would be perilously nearby. Angela waited for the thump of the glass, the drip of water on the vinyl floor. No thump. No drip. Rose had cleared the zinnias and was rasping medicated relief down her windpipe.

Angela flipped off her chair brake and spun briskly toward her roommate. "Way past news time," she chirped as she sailed by Rose's bed. She paused at the open door. "You coming?" From atop her counterpane Rose shook her head, still holding her lungs full of stramonium.

Down the corridor to the rec room, Angela maneuvered her chair like a prize quarter horse, cornering a walker here, a tray rack there. Earlyn Sweetwater Aiken and Mister Ed dozed in their respective chairs before "The City at Noon." Angela scooted between them, turned up the volume, set her brake and took out her knitting. Local newswoman Sonja Lee was leading into the day's human interest story.

"It's a mystery, ladies and gentlemen." Sonja's dark face filled the screen. "The last pup of the sixth litter of dying newborns has just breathed its last at the So-Fine Kennel, for decades one of the country's largest providers of purebred golden retrievers. Mrs. A.H. Henley, a sister-in-law, by the way, of Memphis' mayor, is nonplussed. According to her, there is no rational explanation for this recent rash of sickly puppies."

Mrs. Henley, in crisp Banana Republic togs, spoke earnestly to the camera, and into the microphone held by a disembodied hand. "We've checked every possibility—the mother dogs' diets, their health records, temperature, pollutant levels, the birth process itself, all of it. Everything is normal, all identical to the conditions that surround the litters who live."

"Then there are litters who live?" asked Sonja Lee, now apparent by Mrs. Henley's side as the camera dropped back to a medium shot of the two women.

"Yes. Well, one at least since spring when the phenomenon began. They're here." She guided Sonja to a large well-lighted enclosure full of seven suckling balls of fur.

Angela finished off a front row of a lavender sock. The large reclining dog raised her head to assure viewers that she was a contented mother—bright-eyed, dutiful, enduring, happy. Then a close-up of one slick, tight-eyed pup. Mrs. Henley's well-mani-cured forefinger stroked its nuzzling body. Also clearly content. Angela leaned forward, peering over the tops of her glasses and then settled back again.

"We have even tried this mother as surrogate for some of the failing newborns. They rally for a few hours but then inevitably die. We are stricken, of course." The camera came back to Mrs. Henley and Sonja Lee. "They are such darlings." Her fond hand rested on the mother's neck. "As you can imagine, we've consulted veterinarians from all over the globe, biologists, medical men. None can come up with the answer."

Angela shifted her yarn, glanced down as she started another row, and then turned her attention back to the screen while her fingers flew to the click of the needles. Mr. Ed to her right gurgled in prelude to a full-fledged snore.

Mrs. Henley led the newswoman along immaculate canine quarters. Sonja's voice faded in again. ". . . can't understand why they all aren't dying, why there is one litter that's hale and hearty."

"Indeed," nodded the bereaved kennel owner. She drew the viewer toward a sad canine family scene. "Here's my daughter, Carey," she said, "with Lily's Golden Treasure. This dog is the only one we've bred twice since this started happening. She lost all of her first litter and now it looks like this one is failing too." A jean-clad little girl stood protectively beside a mass of tiny bodies, some breathing heavily, some ominously still. Lily's Golden Treasure sat immobile by the child, noncommittally observing her offspring.

Carey's hand stroked the mother's head, drawing it up as the camera moved in. The great dog face filled the screen. Angela whipped off her glasses and leaned forward. "By crackey!" she ejaculated. She flung her knitting to the floor.

Mr. Ed snapped to attention. "Huh?"

"By crackey what, Angela?" stuttered Earlyn Sweetwater Aiken, her nap demolished. "What's going on? Angela!"

Angela had rolled smack up to the TV and was shaking the box vigorously and in vain. "Let's see that last momma dog again!" she was shouting. "Bring her back!" Technology ignored her. Sonja Lee wound up the day's feature story from her studio desk. "And that's the puzzle of the dying puppies, ladies and gentlemen."

Mr. Ed dropped back into his other world. Earlyn Sweetwater spoke sotto voce, "Angela, hush up. You'll have Tiny and the whole bunch in here!"

Angela composed herself. "Where's the kennels?" she said,

retrieving her knitting.

"Where's what?"

"The kennels. Where's the So-Fine Kennels?" Without waiting for an answer Angela hove about and stopped just short of collision with the big woman in a striped uniform who blocked the doorway.

"Miz Anderson, what's—"

Angela was all smiles. "Ah, Tiny, just an old woman's tantrum. I'm going back to my room."

"We heard you yelling . . ."

"Damn straight. You have to talk back to the television, don't you? It's all over now. No need to worry." She patted Tiny's rump as she squeezed into the hall. "Oh, by the way, where's the So-Fine Kennels? You know, for dogs. What part of town?"

Tiny looked from Angela to her companions. "Never heard of it. They raise dogs up north of town by the new park. That it?"

"Maybe. I'll find a phone book." She was gone.

"Miz Anderson, you know you can't bring up that dog thing again!" Tiny's voice echoed behind her.

It took Angela McBurney Anderson forty-seven seconds to ascertain that Rose Santolla was sleeping peacefully and to plump her own bedclothes into a semblance of a sleeping body. It took her less time than that to hobble on her cane to the bathroom, secure the door behind her, strip out of her bedjacket and gown, and fling open the large window over the commode.

She closed her eyes, stood on tiptoe, and raised her hands high above her head. As she breathed the incantation, she recalled a spider, a snow-clad mountain, and caverns of ice. A thousand bright suns swept from the sky to clothe her frail body, now a perfect vessel, strong and invincible. Soft silver cynclon fabric covered her like a second skin, taut and shining over full eager muscles. Black lasolite boots fitted smoothly, toe to thigh. Black tights and gloves, black crystal tiara set on ash-gray curls, mercury cape of piezoform lightness—all keyed to emblazon the silver "W" on a field of ebony that rode high on her breasts. Using the mirror, she positioned her plain-glass spectacles for the proper grandmotherly look and took up her cane, now a six-foot feather-weight shaft of ferroduct.

She hopped onto the windowsill, smiled at the mimosa tree, stepped upward onto the air, and vanished into the sun.

The Administrator of the Maybrook Convalescent Home heard a cackle as she opened the door of her Honda Accord. When she turned to look, she saw only the mimosa tree waving to a speck in the sky.

Carey Flavia Henley kicked the tire of the blue compact that had nosed onto the side lawn.

"You'd better not do that," her brother's voice cautioned. "It belongs to one of the reporters."

"I don't care. It's almost on the puppies' graves. See?" She pointed to a row of small mounds, each decorated with cut flowers. "And right there," she pointed to the front passenger seat, "is where we're burying two more this afternoon. So get off!" She flung herself fists first at the fender, her voice modulating into a steady wail.

Wee Willy clasped his hands over his ears and trotted toward the house. Carey's cries did not abate. She was, in fact, inhaling for even greater vocal protest when her eye caught the form of a large bird over the top of the trees.

It wasn't a bird. It wasn't a plane, either.

The silver figure drew herself into perpendicular position for a noiseless landing and stood, leaning casually on her staff.

"Hi Carey," she said. "You want the car moved?"

Carey's eyes were wide. She nodded.

"No problem." The old lady bent to get one hand under the frame, then effortlessly lifted the front end of the car off the ground and walked with it to the other side of the driveway, pivoting it entirely clear of the canine graveyard.

"Ooooooooo," breathed Carey, any inclination to laugh now submerged in admiration.

"Will you help me figure out why the puppies are dying?" said the old lady, squatting beside her.

"Oh yes! That would be—but how do you know my name?"

"I saw you on television."

"Who are you?"

"I'm called Wondercrone by those who know and love me best."

"Wondercrone!" The very name was magic. "But my teacher says you're not really real."

"Well, your teacher is wrong. Now can we get to work?" She

handed Carey her long wand.

"Sure." Carey stroked the dull metallic surface. It was cool to her touch.

"Good." Wondercrone blew hard on her glasses and wiped them with the tip of her cape. "Now you understand we have to do this sleuthing in secret? At least 'til we make sure?" Carey nodded. "Good. Now show me all the dogs that lost their puppies."

"Can I carry your stick? Your wand?"

Wondercrone grinned. "Why not? Just don't rub it without asking me first. 'Stood?"

"'Stood." Carey held the sweet power in both her hands and peeped around the back of the automobile. "This way," she gestured and began a crouched stalk around the hydrangea bushes.

Like two culprits they slipped into the kennels, easily avoiding visitors and kennel personnel. "Fancy set-up," muttered Wondercrone, noting that each dog had its own run and its own smaller enclosures for eating and sleeping. Some of the bereaved mother dogs were dozing, some were alert and eager for company. Some kept watch over the world with soft brown eyes.

With a formal whisper, Carey introduced Wondercrone to each dog. The silvered lady addressed each one, asking permission of each to be allowed to hold her. Then, with the dog in her arms, she slipped into a brief stillness that Carey dared not disturb.

"Umm-hummm," mused the old lady after the third dog.

"What is it?"

"Just like I thought."

"What? No fair, Wondercrone. No fair not to tell me."

"Later," mumbled the dame, moving onto another dog.

Carey was leading the way to the abode of one of the great champions of all time, Golden Guinea, when she rounded a corner. There, strolling directly toward them down the corridor of kennels, came her mother with The Press in tow. Mrs. Henley was speaking sadly of the loss to her three listeners. Carey gasped and backed up into Wondercrone.

"Shhhsh," said the old lady, holding her close. Then as she began guiding the girl back the way they had come, Carey gasped again and clutched the old lady's silver-clad thigh. Wee Willie was galloping down the row of enclosures toward them intent on finding his mother.

"Trapped!" Wondercrone hissed. "Hand me the wand." Then,

holding the stick, vertically in front of them both, she moved it in a circle around the two of them.

Carey heard strange names and the words ". . . in Her Triple Aspects," and stared as Wee Willie ran right by them, inches away, without a glance. He pounded around the corner shouting "Momma!"

Mrs. Henley paused in her discourse.

"Momma! Carey's kicking the shit out of . . ."

"Willie!" Mrs. Henley drew her son to her side with a little jerk.

"Well, she is. She's beatin' up on your car, Mister. You better move it."

"We're almost finished anyway, and then we'll be going right back to the car. Why don't you just come with us, Willie?" She graciously maneuvered her guests toward Wondercrone and Carey, guiding Willie along with them and constructing a smooth peroration about the unfortunate circumstances. "So we don't know what we shall do yet . . ."

As the group passed a few feet away from Wondercrone and the small girl, one of the reporters stopped and looked their way. He frowned, and then shook his head and fell into step behind his hostess. "We may indeed have to close down the So-Fine Kennels," she was saying. "And what a tragedy that would be—"

"Whew!" breathed Carey as Wondercrone whipped the stick around them again, this time the opposite way, and with an opposite incantation. "That was wonderful."

Wondercrone grinned and peered over the top of her spectacles. "Come on. Let's find those other dogs."

When they'd interviewed the last bereaved canine, Wondercrone sat back on her haunches. "Well, that's at least half of it," she said. "Dam's Dander, just like I thought."

"Dam's what?" Carey sat back on her haunches beside Wondercrone.

"Carey my girl, are there any females not bred yet?"

"You mean that aren't mothers?"

"No, I mean that have not been with a pappa dog at all. Any that haven't been pregnant?"

"Sure. All the girl dogs over a year can have puppies. And we don't sell them all. We keep the best of the litters to make more babies."

"Take me to them," said the old woman, rising.

In the enclosures where younger females were kept together, Carey pointed out the ones she knew the kennel would keep for breeding. Wondercrone sat with each one, studying her closely. Then she held each one as she had the older dogs, and on releasing them, nodded. "Here, my girl," she directed, "hold this little beauty like I just did."

Carey settled beside the frisky subject, trying to calm her.

"You got to be firm," said the old woman. "Put your arms all the way around her. Touch as much of her as you can with your arms and hands and chest. Good. Now lay your head next to hers and squeeze just ever-so-firmly. Not too hard now. Good. How does it feel?

"She's safe. She feels safe."

"Good. Now Carey, do a little experiment. Think about puppies. Think about *her* puppies. Make a picture in your mind of her having a big litter of little ones. Make them real in your mind. Do you understand?"

Carey nodded, closed her eyes. The dog sat patiently, then began to twitch. Her tail began a wide swing, back and forth, back and forth. "She likes it. She wants to do it now!"

"Fine," said Wondercrone. "Now try Goldenrod here. Give her the same treatment."

Dutifully Carey soothed the next dog into her body grip and closed her eyes once more. This time the reaction was different. The animal became agitated, even shivered. She tried to break from Carey's grasp. "Oh, she hates it!" said the child. "She doesn't want to do that at all! See? Oh, she's not happy."

"Calm her down then. Take away the picture of her puppies."

The dog was soothed. In the next few minutes, under the old woman's direction, Carey hugged a dozen dogs, nine of them unhappy in the same way Goldenrod had been. Both the experimenters had a time calming the animals, so intense was their reaction.

"Well," said Wondercrone, "that tells the story, doesn't it?"

"Wondercrone, these doggies don't *want* to have puppies. At least most of them don't."

"Ummm. I figured as much when I saw Lily's Golden Treasure on the tube. She had a look in her eye. The Dam's Dander look. Means she had a grudge about having to have the pups. A big grudge. So big that the pups up and died. And these girls here, these future mothers, most of them will get the Dam's Dander look if you make them have babies they don't want."

"And their puppies will die."

"Probably."

"Then we mustn't make them have puppies."

"Your momma's not going to like that idea."

Two of the younger dogs lolled on their backs. Carey stroked them. "Wondercrone, it's not Dam's Dander yet, but even these dogs are trying to tell us something. Look here." She held up one head. "There's a look in her eye, too, if you can just see it."

"Umm-hmm. That's the warning look. Virgin's Eye, they used to call it. Look at Goldenrod. She's got it. Virgin's Eye if ever I saw it. In fact, only three of these younger girls don't have it, right?"

Carey was doing her own investigation. "Right. But Wondercrone, lots of dogs must have had pups they didn't want. And the pups didn't die. Why are they dying now?"

"I don't know. Rebellion in the dog kingdom, maybe."

"Maybe things just got so bad they had to do something awful to make us pay attention."

"Maybe." Wondercrone stood up, picked up her staff. "Well, what do you say we find your momma?"

"Well, Wondercrone," sighed Mrs. A.H. Henley, still amidst The Press, "this is quite a theory. If I were not at my wit's end I probably couldn't believe it."

"You got a perfectly good way to test it right here." Wondercrone put her hand on her young cohort's shoulder. "Just let Carey talk to the dogs. She can tell you which ones you can breed."

"Our production—" She looked uneasily at the note-scrawling reporters. "I mean, we won't be able to meet the demand if we're breeding fewer dogs . . ."

"But Momma, the dogs we do have will be so much happier!" Carey held Wondercrone's hand.

"Well, there is that," said her mother.

"Wondercrone," urged one of the newsmen, raising his camera. "Can I get a shot—?"

"Negative. I've got to be gone." She hugged Carey.

Mrs. Henley raised her voice. "But how do we thank you?"

"You might give a dog or two to the old folks' homes around town. They need some pressure to let them have animals there. Give them those girls that would rather not have puppies." With that the silvered old lady lifted Carey and swung her into her mother's surprised arms. "Thank you, Carey, my girl. 'Twas a fine day."

She raised her stick in farewell and stepped up on the air. A moment later she was a dot in the sky heading south.

Rose Santolla pounded on the bathroom door. "Angela!" she wheezed. "You been in there all afternoon. Angela!"

"I'm coming, Rose, I'm coming." Angela's voice was very loud.

"I need to get in there. What're you doing? Angela, if you don't open this door I'll get Tiny—"

Angela hobbled out of the bathroom, leaning heavily on her cane. "Doing? I been doing my business. What else you do in the bathroom?" She brushed past Rose and collapsed in her chair.

"Well you don't have to take all day." Rose was about to close the door.

"Rose, are you allergic to dogs?"

"Am I what? No, of course not. I love dogs." She slammed the door behind her.

"Good," smiled Angela, cocking her head to look at the mimosa tree. She breathed on her glasses and wiped them with her satin bed jacket. "That's good."

A Sweet Crime

Rose Million Healey

What's wrong with this picture, I asked myself?

"Classy Clarissa's Redneck Roots" the caption sneered. It was an ordinary enough family photograph taken some twenty years ago. A working class mother and father stood stiffly posed with their adult son and daughter. Something about the group bothered me. What?

I dropped the magazine onto my desk. Who was I kidding? Probably what was bothering me was my conscience. Instead of typing reports, I'd been indulging my appetite for gossip. Slick scandal sheets are like potato chips to me: I know they're a reprehensible habit, but every so often I get this craving.

At least this time I did have an excuse. The gaudy cover of *Strictly Personal* had promised "Shocking Truths Behind the Wallace Case." My former boss, Lt. Francis X. Foyle of the NYPD, was in charge of that one. Eventually, he'd be coming around to discuss it with me, either gloating because he'd solved it or hinting for help because he hadn't. If the latter, I wanted to be prepared with as much background material as possible. Not that Foyle would ever actually ask for my assistance. He hasn't done that since I quit the force to start Ade's Detective Agency.

When the murder of Clarissa Wallace's brother initially hit the headlines a couple of weeks ago, I'd been too busy to do more than scan the story. April is the cruelest month at Ade's. We specialize in tracing runaways, and the first warm rains of the year always bring a deluge of AWOL's. Don't ask me why. Perhaps the poetic mixing of memory and desire triggers restlessness. Perhaps it's just spring fever.

Anyway, before consulting *Strictly Personal*, I'd known only the basic facts concerning the Wallace/Plymouth affair. Mrs. Clarissa Wallace, a wealthy "patron of the arts," had received a box of candy in the mail. Being a devout dieter, she had resisted temptation. Her brother, one Norman Plymouth, sampled the goodies and promptly turned up his toes. Norman's autopsy and an analysis of the remaining chocolates had revealed enough rat poison to purify the entire city of Hamelin. It was assumed that Mrs. Wallace had been the intended target.

In the newspaper and television accounts I'd seen there'd been scant speculation as to possible suspects or motives. With lipsmacking relish *Strictly Personal* had supplied the missing details. Deftly skirting all libel laws, the article named some Beautiful People who had turned ugly when dealing with Clarissa Wallace. The lady herself was described as a pushy *parvenu*.

Two years ago, Mrs. Wallace had been Clara Plymouth, a fortyish practical nurse from Alaska. Very practical, as it turned out. She'd married her rich, elderly patient, Heston Wallace II, and shortly thereafter inherited the bulk of his estate.

Understandably, this had not endeared her to the erstwhile heirs. Helena and Heston Wallace III had maintained a dignified public reticence concerning their upstart stepmother. However, *Strictly Personal* reported "on good authority" that the two blue bloods loathed Clarissa and wished her dead.

There were others, the article insinuated, harboring similar sentiments.

Gwen Rickenbry, a prominent socialite, had been feuding bitterly with Clarissa over who was the hostess with the mostest. The famous couturier, Andre Corbeau, was suing Clarissa for slander. And an exotic dancer, stage-named Nefra Titty, claimed Clarissa had blighted her romance with Norman Plymouth.

Ah, murder in the *haut monde* with five glamorous suspects. The case was certainly intriguing.

A lot more intriguing than typing reports, I decided, and grabbed up the magazine again.

Pictures of the *dramatis personae* were splashed across a two-page spread. I studied each one carefully. Norman Plymouth hadn't rated an individual shot. The only picture of him was the one that included his parents and sister. I'd already noted that, two decades ago, the victim had been a pudge in his twenties with shifty blue eyes and a hangdog demeanor.

Moving along to the touched-up studio portrait of Clarissa, I saw what looked like a real Queen of Mean. Artful lighting and an airbrush hadn't managed to soften her hard mouth and black, beady eyes. I felt inclined to sympathize with her enemies.

However, the enemies didn't seem particularly sympathetic when you got right down to it. Helena and Heston Wallace III, captured by the camera at a charity ball, wore an air of icy superiority that suggested they could be cruel if crossed. The same went for the smirking dress designer and haughty hostess. As for the dancer, Nefra Titty, she seemed even more formidable than the others. A publicity-still showed her conquering a cobra.

Judging by facial expressions alone, the whole lot of them looked capable of posting a lethal box of bonbons to a rival. I sighed. I was getting nowhere fast. As if drawn by a magnet, my attention strayed back to the Plymouth family photograph. Why did it nag at me?

According to *Strictly Personal*, the picture had been stolen from Norman Plymouth's bedroom by one of their reporters. Disguised as a repairman, he'd sneaked in and found it slipped behind a framed close-up of Nefra Titty. The discovery had been considered quite a *coup*, mainly because Norman had written, "Ma, Pa, Clara and Me 6/18/71" on the back of the picture. Snidely, the article pointed out that the picture and the date proved Clarissa Wallace was neither as well-born nor as young as she pretended.

Unfortunately, it didn't prove anything to me except that I was wasting time. I decided to give up on the picture. Maybe something would come to me later. Meanwhile, I was hot to reread the text. The time had come, I thought, to apply my Method.

The Method is what I call my system for tackling a case. Like a frustrated actress, I cast myself in each of the leading roles. Foyle pooh-poohs the idea, but by imagining I *am* a certain person, I can sometimes figure out if he or she is guilty.

The Norman Plymouth murder, with its juicy range of characters, was just my meat. Pouring over the pages of *Strictly Personal*, I got so deeply absorbed in Methodizing, I failed to notice that my privacy had been invaded.

"Ho, Thelma," an all-too-familiar voice rasped. "Improving your mind, are you?"

Curses. Caught with my low literary taste hanging out. Foyle's sardonic smile told me it was too late to camouflage *Strictly Personal* behind *Roget's Thesaurus* or some other worthy tome.

"Don't you ever knock?" I complained.

"What? And give you a chance to pretend you're working?" Foyle helped himself to coffee from the hot plate on the windowsill.

He was freshly shaven and presentably attired. A bad sign. When the Lieutenant doesn't resemble Columbo after a rainstorm, it means he's on top of a case and intends to lord it over me.

Sauntering to a chair, he plopped down. "No matter what that rag says," he pointed to my magazine, "the stripper's guilty. I'll bet my bottom dollar on it."

"Didn't you lose that on the Tyson-Douglas match?" I asked.

Foyle ignored the gibe. "It's open-and-shut, Thel. Clarissa Wallace wouldn't let her brother marry a stripper, so the stripper tried to poison her. The dumb broad bumped her boyfriend off by mistake."

Having formed a few hazy opinions of my own, I said, "Nobody's that dumb."

"You haven't met Nefra." Foyle rolled his eyes skyward. "The I.Q. of a pancake. Besides," he added, "murderers *are* dumb. If they weren't, they'd find some other solution to their problems."

"Mrs. Wallace seems to be a problem for a lot of folks," I said.

"Yours truly included. Two interviews with her and I'm ready for early retirement. That woman's got all the charm of a stopped up sink." He grimaced. "I kind of hate to put Nefra out of circulation. Anybody wanting to kill Clarissa Wallace can't be all bad."

"What makes you so sure the dancer's your perp?"

Shrugging, Foyle slipped into officialese: "A meticulous sifting of the evidence."

I couldn't let him get away with that. "Come off it, Francis. There isn't any evidence."

"Sez who?" he bristled.

"Sez *Strictly Personal*. They pumped a 'reliable source' in your office." I ticked off the facts on my fingers. "Easily obtained poison. Ordinary candy. No fingerprints on the box or wrappings.

You haven't even got handwriting or typing clues. The killer cut Mrs. Wallace's name and address from a piece of her own stationery and taped it to the package. So much for your *evidence!*"

"Wait'll I get hold of that 'source,'" Foyle fumed. "I'll rip—"

Foyle gets pretty graphic when contemplating disciplinary tactics. I thought it best to interrupt. "Have you read the article?"

"—his guts out and ram—Huh?"

Slowly, I repeated my question. Foyle's cheeks faded from puce to their customary mauve. "Sure, I read it. Damned la-dee-dah snoops. Think they know everything."

"What do you know that they don't?" I leaned forward. "For instance, how about the murderee? *Strictly Personal* doesn't give him much space."

"Well, they wouldn't, would they? He wasn't highfalutin enough. You can be damned sure *we* ran a thorough check on him." Pulling a dog-eared notebook from his pocket, Foyle tossed it to me.

Deciphering the hen scratches, I read Norman Plymouth's statistics:

Male, Caucasian, 44 yrs., 5' 9", 230 lbs., brown hair, blue eyes, no visible scars. Petty con man and suspected blackmailer. Originally from Alaska. Drifted down to the Lower Forty-Eight circa 1976. Mostly West Coast operations. Occasional brush with the law. No convictions. *No known enemies.*

Arrived N.Y.C. six weeks prior to his death. Moved in with sister, Clara Plymouth Wallace. Activities during that time legal, if unsavory. Frequented O.T.B. parlors and SoHo dives. Consorted with Imogene Greblin (a.k.a. Nefra Titty) belly ballerina at sleazy Glitz Club.

"Not an ideal relative for someone aiming at the *Social Register,*" I remarked, looking up. "Clarissa Wallace must have loved having that low-lifer hanging around her neck."

As a matter of fact, she did," Foyle said. "Hard-hearted Hannah had her soft spot, and Norman was it. Seems he was all the family she had. Their parents are dead. When he turned up, she took him in, gave him a big allowance and even made out a will in his favor. Her secretary—eh, pardon me—Mrs. Wallace's Personal Assistant—said Clarissa treated her brother like royalty."

I remembered reading that Clarissa's elegant secretary had discovered the body.

On the morning of the poisoning, she and Mrs. Wallace had dealt with the mail, which included the now infamous box of chocolates. The peculiarly addressed parcel aroused some curiosity, she said, but the candy had proved to be "too, too plebeian." Since no card was enclosed, Mrs. Wallace had dismissed the gift as an advertisement of some sort. She'd pushed it aside, saying it might be suitable for the servants. The unopened box had been on her desk when the two women left the library.

At noon they had attended a fashion show luncheon. Mrs. Wallace went on to a concert at Lincoln Center. The secretary returned to the mansion around two o'clock.

Her tender sensibilities had been greatly offended by the sight awaiting her. Sprawled on the library floor was the lifeless body of Norman Plymouth.

The servants, having been in the kitchen watching soap operas, had heard nothing before she alerted them.

"Who saw Norman that day? The day he was killed," I asked Foyle.

"No one. He spent the morning in his room. The guy was a night owl. Usually snoozed until noon or later."

"What did the coroner say about time of death?"

"Between noon and two p.m. Ate the candy on an empty stomach. Doc thinks Plymouth went into convulsions within minutes. Wouldn't have been able to yell or run for help."

"Poor guy."

"Yeah, well, there aren't many mourning for him except his sister. The others we talked to couldn't have cared less. Norman's SoHo chums summed him up as a 'nosy, greedy slob.' The Wallace staff said ditto—in more refined language. Nobody seemed surprised at how he died. Plymouth had a reputation for poking around where he didn't belong and for eating whatever he could get his hands on. I got the distinct impression that he won't be sorely missed."

"Nefra says she'll miss him," I argued.

"She'll miss her freedom more when I get through with her," Foyle said grimly.

"You still haven't told me why you're so sure she's the perp,"

I pointed out. "How come you've zeroed in on her?"

Faking surprise, Foyle raised his eyebrows. "Didn't *Strictly Personal* cover that?"

"You know damned well it didn't."

"Awe, what a shame." Abruptly, he dropped the sarcasm and hunched toward me. "Yesterday I hauled Nefra in. Gave her a polite third degree. She admitted knowing Norman was Clarissa's heir. *And* that he'd written mash notes to her *on his sister's stationery.*" Foyle tipped back in his chair, looking very pleased with himself. "Nefra had the means to address the package plus a great incentive for sending it. All that stood between her and a pot of gold was Clarissa Wallace. Means and motive, Thelma. Means and motive. What more do you need?"

"A little proof might be useful."

"Don't worry, we'll get the proof." Waving his arms airily, Foyle tipped his chair so far back the laws of gravity were severely strained. "Nefra's a diabetic. Our lab's testing her syringes for traces of chocolate or poison. Her bills are being gone over, too. Buying the murder weapon on credit's the kind of ditsy thing she'd do. If we come up empty there, we'll canvas the stores selling that brand of candy. Nefra's no plain Jane, you know. Foot-high hairdo, three-inch fingernails and a lot of vavoom in between. Some clerk's bound to remember waiting on her." He grinned. "We may not have to bother. She's so crazy to see her name in the papers, she'll probably confess."

"Even if she does, I won't believe it," I said.

"Why not? It's clear as—" Foyle brought the chair down with a hard smack. He smacked his forehead even harder. "Oh, God. You've been *playacting* again. I suppose Nefra's innocent because she doesn't *feel* guilty to you.

"Well, she doesn't."

"Okay, who *does*?" he demanded. "It better not be Corbeau or the Rickenbry woman. They were in Europe when the chocolates were mailed."

"That doesn't surprise me," I said. It was true. The designer and the hostess had never seemed to be serious contenders. I figured *Strictly Personal* had tossed their names in for their celebrity value.

"Okay. *You* surprise *me*," Foyle challenged. "Astound me with that Method of yours. Go on, tell me who did it."

Wouldn't I have loved to? I was pretty sure who didn't do it. The two Wallaces, I'd eliminated almost immediately. The logical time for Heston III or Helena to off Clarissa would have been before their daddy married her, not two years later. What would they gain now? Revenge?

Placing myself in their aristocratic shoes, I'd felt far too fastidious to mess around with a vendetta involving cheap candy and rat poison. Besides, they hadn't contested Clarissa's inheritance nor indulged in petty squabbles with her. It was hardly likely they would risk their dignity, not to mention a jail sentence, at this late date.

With the Wallaces, Corbeau and Rickenbry stricken from the list, only Nefra remained. I tried her on for size and found she didn't fit the crime. Not this particular crime. The *modus operandi* was wrong. Pushing poison into dozens of chocolates would require digital dexterity and patience. Nefra had three-inch fingernails and seemed an impetuous type. While casting myself in the role of the dancer, I'd had an urge to sic my snake on Clarissa. Concocting a complicated murder scheme simply wasn't her style.

Of course, I might be mistaken about her temperament, and the nails could be false. Even so, I thought Nefra should be ruled out. Sending poison to the Wallace house where her lover might get at it was too incredibly stupid. From the start I'd been convinced of that, and Foyle's theories hadn't changed my opinion. Every instinct told me the dancer wasn't guilty.

So where did that leave me? Up the creek without a suspect, that's where. Unless—

All along, there had been another possibility . . . .

"Why the long silence?" Foyle inquired. "The old Method getting rusty, is it?"

"Not rusty, just aimed in the wrong direction," I said. "Listen, Francis, what we've got here is a killer smart enough to plan a clueless crime. Wouldn't he or she be too smart to kill the wrong person? Couldn't the poison have been meant for Norman Plymouth?"

"Brilliant." Foyle clapped his hands in ironic slow motion. "What'll you do for an encore? Invent the wheel? Hell, we sniffed that trail to a dead end a week ago. Who'd benefit? Plymouth didn't have a dime, and nobody cared enough about him to kill him." He shook his head. "Naw, Clarissa was the target, and

Nefra's the baby who aimed at her."

"Nefra. Always Nefra. You've got a one-track mind."

"Better that than a derailed one. Admit it, kiddo, you're stumped."

God, I hate it when he's right.

"You and your *Strictly Personal* approach," he gloated, rubbing it in. "Two bucks down the drain."

I'd paid two-fifty, but why correct him? My defeat was ignominious enough as it was. I glared at the offending periodical. All I'd gotten for my two-fifty was a bunch of worthless pictures . . .

That reminded me. The Plymouth family photograph.

As I began thumbing through *Strictly Personal*, Foyle stood up. "Isn't this where I came in?"

"Give me a couple minutes more," I mumbled.

Sighing a long-suffering sigh, he sat down again.

I ought to let go. Foyle had a reasonable case against Nefra. I had nothing. Stubbornly, I continued to examine "Classy Clarissa's Redneck Roots."

Wearing a dowdy white dress, Clarissa was almost unrecognizable. Time, money and a nose job had altered every feature except her mean mouth and snake's eyes. Standing at her left was Mrs. Plymouth who had squeezed herself into a bright floral print. On Clarissa's right, plump Norman and his plump father stood, sporting identical dark suits; white flowers drooped in their lapels.

I'd seen happier faces at funerals. The older couple's watery blue gaze was stern and humorless. Norman seemed ready to burst into tears. Only Clarissa looked vaguely pleased. What occasion had this grim quartet been commemorating? A birthday? A graduation? June 18, 1971 . . .

"Give up. Thelma," Foyle said impatiently. "You can stare at that crummy magazine till your eyes drop out, but—"

I stopped listening. He'd said the magic word. Suddenly, I knew what was wrong with the picture. The eyes. Of course, the eyes.

I squeezed my own eyes shut and watched a whole new scenario unfold. Quickly, I played one more role . . .

The pieces of the puzzle fell beautifully into place.

As Foyle's foot began tapping the floor, I opened my eyes. "Have you considered the possibility that—Clarissa poisoned Norman?"

Foyle snorted. "I'm considering the possibility that you're crazy. Why would she kill her brother?"

"*Was* he her brother? Did you ever bother to check?"

"Why should I?" he blustered. "I—I—"

"You took it for granted. Everybody did. Clarissa and Norman said they were brother and sister. Why question it? But what if they were married instead?"

"Where'd that bright idea come from? More playacting?"

"Partly," I admitted, "and partly from this." I trotted over to Foyle and shoved *Strictly Personal* into his hands. "See the eyes in that picture? Mr. and Mrs. Plymouth's are blue. Clarissa's are almost black."

"So? You object to the color scheme?"

"I object to accepting her as Norman's sister. High school biology taught me that two blue-eyed people can't produce a dark-eyed child. The Plymouth's weren't Clarissa's parents."

Unimpressed, Foyle yawned. "Ever hear of adoption?"

"Sure," I conceded, "that's one explanation, but that picture has 'wedding' written all over it. Clarissa's wearing white. The men are duded up with flowers in their lapels. An obviously poor family doesn't pay for a professional photograph unless it's an important event in their lives. The date is June 18, 1971. June. People get married in June—"

"People do a lot of things in June," Foyle snapped, handing the magazine back to me. "Even if Clarissa and Norman were married—and I'm not saying they were—what difference would it make?"

I took a deep breath and threw my bombshell. "Wouldn't it make a difference if Clarissa committed bigamy when she married Heston Wallace?"

I'd expected an explosion, and Foyle didn't disappoint me.

"What!" he yelped. "Of all the damned conclusion-jumping—"

"It's a logical conclusion," I broke in. "If Clarissa and Norman had been divorced—"

"*If* they'd been married! *If* they'd been divorced!"

"Don't burst a blood vessel," I yelled. "Hear me out. Then have a fit if you want to."

Clamping his mouth shut, Foyle glared at me.

I started talking as fast as I knew how. "*If* they'd been divorced, Clarissa wouldn't have passed Norman off as her brother.

She'd have sent him packing. An *ex*-husband was no threat. But a living, legal spouse could have cost her a fortune. Don't you get it? Her marriage to Wallace wasn't legal. *Norman was blackmailing Clarissa*."

"You're off in the wild blue yonder," Foyle grumbled. "You've got no proof." He'd calmed down. He was listening.

"Norman must have been blackmailing her," I insisted. "Why else would a social-climber like Clarissa take a petty criminal into her house and make out a will in his favor?"

"Yeah." Foyle rubbed his chin. "Come to think of it, that sisterly love stuff she spouted did seem out of character."

That was all the encouragement I needed. I was off and running. "The way I see it, Norman and Clarissa split up in 1976. That's when your notes said Norman left Alaska. Either he deserted her, or she kicked him out; it doesn't matter. We know he went to the West Coast, and she came to New York. They lost touch. When Clarissa met Heston Wallace, the old guy was dying. Clarissa didn't have time to locate Norman and divorce him. Maybe she thought he was dead. Maybe she just took a chance he wouldn't find out she'd married money."

"He did find out, though, and moved in on her," Foyle said.

"Right. There they were, living under the same roof. It was just a question of time before one of them did the other in. Norman probably had plans for killing Clarissa and collecting on that will, but she beat him to the punch. A former nurse would be pretty sure to have an old syringe handy, or know how to get one, and rat poison's easy to come by. She knew her victim was greedy and nosy. So she mailed herself a sweet present, and let Norman's nature take it's course!"

I suddenly realized I'd been pacing up and down like a prosecuting attorney. Halting in front of Foyle, I said, "Okay, your honor. I rest my case. What's the verdict? Is it worth a call to the Department of Records in Alaska? I—"

Foyle was already reaching for the telephone.

A short time later, we had the results. Ah, the miracle of modern technology. An Alaskan computer confirmed that, in the village of Beatle Bluff, Norman Kenneth Plymouth, bachelor, had pledged his troth to Clara Mae Ludloe, spinster, on June 18, 1971. Said computer failed to locate any record of a divorce.

Foyle and I digested the data in silence for a few minutes.

76

Finally, I said, "Clarissa's going to be a tough nut to crack."

"I've cracked tougher," he assured me, buttoning his coat. "That syringe you mentioned might still be hidden in her house, you know. Or maybe *she* bought the candy with a credit card. One way or another, I'll get her."

An old bloodhound on the trail, he lumbered to his feet and started toward the door. "She slipped up somewhere; they all do. Like I told you, Thelma, murderers are stupid."

"You also told me Nefra was the murderer." I couldn't resist reminding him.

His hand on the doorknob, Foyle turned. Not quite facing me, he said, "Awe, you didn't think I was serious about that, did you? Hell, I was just testing you. Clarissa's been my prime suspect all along."

As my mouth dropped open, he shut the door behind him.

Francis X. Foyle had the last word. Again.

In a world fraught with uncertainties, it's rather comforting to know that some things never change.

The Ice Bag in Question

Nancy R. Herndon

"Maude Crowder won't be at the meeting tonight," said Detective Sergeant Elena Jarvis as she eyed the spindly chairs, the pink tablecloths, and the French travel posters of Cafe de Orleans. "She was brought into the hospital last night in a coma."

"Good Lord! What happened?" asked Sarah Tolland. Maude was a member of their divorced women's support group.

"Well, her husband Alden—and incidentally, it turns out he hates to be called Alden." Elena's expression and tone were sardonic. "Alden's one of the good old boys. Drives a pickup truck. Keeps a shotgun in the rack. Wants everyone to call him Buck. You know the type."

"Not really," said Sarah. "You say he *wants* to be called Buck? Good grief."

"Exactly. Anyway, this Alden *says* she fell down the stairs. The doctor agrees that her head injury probably came from a fall, but she has these . . . these *places* around the hairline. I've never seen anything like it, and neither had he. The skin is—" Elena tried to find a way to describe it "—*gone*! Patches are just gone, and even on top of her head, some of the hair is missing. None of that could come from a fall."

"Ladies." Their waiter bowed. "I am Pierre, your waiter for the evening. Eef I may make a suggestion, ze *escargot* ees especially deleecious tonight."

"*Escargot*? That's snails, right?" asked Elena.

The waiter bowed again. "*Oui*, madam."

"Had any trouble with your *escargot* exploding?"

"Madam, ze *escargot*, zey nevair explode!" exclaimed the waiter, horrified.

"That's what you think." The two women looked at one another and started to laugh because they had met when Sarah's ex-husband charged her with attempting to kill him by exploding a snail on his plate during dinner.

"I'll have steak," said Elena.

"*Oui*, madam," said the offended waiter. "We 'ave Steak Diane, Steak *Au Poivre* —"

"How about steak with chilis?"

"Zat we do not 'ave, madam," he replied stiffly.

"His name is *not* Pierre," said Elena once they had ordered. "My father's got about forty cousins south of the Rio Grande who'd sound just like him if they were trying to pass themselves off as French waiters."

"The chef, fortunately, *is* from France," replied Sarah, who had chosen the restaurant because she loved French food, especially if she didn't have to cook it herself. "Now, you were telling me about Maude. How does her husband explain the missing hair and skin?"

"He says she must have tried to dye her hair and botched it, which sounds unlikely. Maude's hair usually looks like she hasn't bothered to comb it, much less do anything more time-consuming."

"She shouldn't have stayed in the same house with him after she filed for divorce," said Sarah. "Of course, if he had criminal designs on her, it's understandable that he'd want her to, and it was his idea that they continue to share the house."

"So you don't think I'm paranoid for suspecting that he had something to do with the fall—or whatever happened to her?"

"Well, I've never met the man, but anyone who wants people to call him *Buck* . . ." Sarah's eyebrows rose in an amused arch. "And Maude says he was unfaithful. Besides which, we know he's greedy. She started that business, but they'll both end up penniless if he gets the property split he wants."

"I didn't realize that. She must have mentioned it while I was out chasing another drive-by shooter." Elena considered greed a prosecutable motive for attempted murder; Alden Crowder wanted the whole business instead of half, so he shoved Maude downstairs. "Now I'm *sure* I want to find out what really happened."

She took a taste of the soup Sarah had recommended. Pretty bad, but Elena had tasted worse—like the venison *caldillo* her ex-husband Frank used to make. Frank refused to use *jalapenos,* so his *caldillo* was just about as boring as this French stuff, which hadn't even been warmed up.

"First, I need to look around their house," Elena resumed, "check the bathroom for hair dye and medication. Alden claims she took stuff for headaches that made her dizzy—the point being we're supposed to think she fell downstairs because of her medication."

"Can you just go into their house and conduct a search?"

"Well, he won't be there to complain. Alden's down at the hospital acting like he's lost his one true love. The hypocrite! He refuses to leave her bedside. Probably afraid she'll wake up and accuse him of pushing her downstairs. But since tomorrow's Saturday, the kids will be home." She watched Sarah spread some disgusting brown paste on a cracker. "Tell you what. We'll offer to look after the kids. Then you can take them somewhere while I search the house."

"Elena—"

"Since I don't have a search warrant, I'll need about three hours to really toss the place without Alden noticing that I've done it."

"That surely isn't legal, and what am I supposed to do with the children for three hours?"

"Take them to the mall or something."

"I've never spent any time with children. I have no expertise in that area."

"For God's sake, Sarah, it's not as if I'm asking you to build an intercontinental ballistic missile."

"I'll try my hand at the missile," Sarah offered wryly. She was the Chairman of Electrical Engineering at the local university.

Elena laughed. "Thanks, but I don't need a missile this weekend. I do need a baby-sitter, and baby-sitting doesn't take expertise, just patience. Take it from someone who had lots of younger brothers and sisters."

"In that case, I'll search Maude's house for clues, and you can entertain the children."

"Sarah, you wouldn't know a clue if it popped up on your computer screen flagged *I'm a clue*. Now be a friend, and get them out of the house for me. Two o'clock. And Sarah, once they get to like you—"

"Why should they like me?"

"—once they like you, ask them about last night."

"Now let me be sure I understand you correctly, Elena. You want me to insinuate myself into the confidence of two unsuspecting children so that I can interrogate them?"

"Right."

"While you conduct an illegal search of their house?"

"I wouldn't put it that way. If it makes you feel better, I'll do a little dusting while I'm there. You know—help good ole *macho* Alden out with the housework."

"How old are these children?"

"The girl's four; the boy's seven."

Sarah groaned.

A methodical and scholarly person, Sarah Tolland approached her afternoon with the Crowder children as she would a research project. This one seemed to call for expert advice, so she consulted several colleagues, those who were parents. The consensus among electrical engineering professors was that Insights, the children's science museum, offered an exciting and educational experience for youngsters, which sounded reasonable to Sarah. She then read two articles on child psychology, recommended by a friend in the field, and considered herself moderately well prepared for the assignment, if somewhat apprehensive.

"Is it going to explode?" asked Bucky as Sarah demonstrated the Vandergraaff Generator exhibit.

"No, Bucky," said Sarah, "it is not going to explode." Poor child. Had his father actually saddled him with the diminutive of such a ridiculous nickname? "What you're seeing is static electricity, not an incipient explosion. Please stop jumping on the scale, Beth. You'll upset the balance mechanism."

Bo-o-on-ng went the Fairbanks scale as the four-year-old bounced again, trampoline-style. "Look at me!" she squealed and dissolved into giggles as one unlaced sneaker flew into the air and landed on the keyboard of a computer display, causing green and red helicopters to run wild on the screen. Sarah scooped her off the weighing platform, retrieved the sneaker, and restored it to Beth's foot, tying it on with a triple knot. Then she dragged Bucky away from the increasingly chaotic activities of the red and green helicopters and deposited both children in front of a plasma ball that was spewing peach and violet light rays.

"Plasma is the fourth state of matter," Sarah said, breathless from her exertions.

"Are the helicopters going to blow up?" asked Bucky.

"No, not unless the computer does." She took a deep breath and glanced at Beth, who was trying to untie her sneaker. The child didn't seem to have much interest in plasma physics. Perhaps she had been brainwashed into believing that little girls were not supposed to be scientifically inclined. Sarah now wished that she had accepted the museum docent's offer to explain the exhibits. No doubt the woman knew how to make science attractive to minors. Still, Sarah admonished herself, one shouldn't pass up an opportunity to broaden feminine aspirations. "Just think, Beth," she pointed out temptingly, "if you pay attention today, you might grow up to be a physicist."

"I wanna be a daddy when I grow up," said Beth, who had given up on her shoelaces.

"I'll be a physicist," Bucky offered.

The museum docent was frantically pushing computer keys, trying to turn off the alarm bells and erase the exploding helicopters on the screen.

"A daddy?" Although Sarah had always subscribed to the idea that a woman could be anything she wanted to be, she realized that her convictions had just been circumvented by a four-year-old. Perhaps the child had some unusual psychological problem. Confused sexual identification had not been mentioned in either of the articles Sarah had read, and she couldn't think of an appropriate response. Bucky solved that problem.

"Beth's only four," he whispered into Sarah's ear. "So don't tell her she can't be a daddy. It'd pro'bly hurt her feelings."

"Oh." That was a rather sensitive remark for a seven-year-old named Bucky, and he did seem to be interested in science. If only he weren't so *noisy*! The docent had already complained twice about unnecessary shouting and now looked decidedly ill-tempered about Beth's sneaker attack on the computer. This excursion was fast winning a place on Sarah's list of things she never wanted to do again. Right up there with attending rock concerts, judging high school science fairs, and sitting through public readings by her ex-husband of his first volume of verse, *Phallic Fancies*.

"My best friend, Fernie del Valle, has a lamp in his room that looks like that," said Bucky, pressing his nose to the glass that surrounded the plasma exhibit. "It's cool."

"Hot," Sarah corrected, grateful for the return to a scientific topic. "Plasma is ionized gas that exists at temperatures around fifty thousand degrees Fahrenheit."

"Wow!" said Bucky. "I'd better warn him. Fernie's mom gets mad when we drop potato chips on her carpet. She'd probably make him stop watching TV for the rest of his life if that lamp broke and burned down her house." Bucky eyed the plasma display as if he expected it to burst into flames. "Daddy has funny ice that makes fog. I bet it's fifty thousand degrees too 'cause it'll take the skin right off your hands if you touch it."

"That's dry ice," said Sarah. "It's cold, not hot." Alden Crowder had dry ice? At home?

"When I grow up to be a daddy, I'll have funny ice too," said Beth. "An' I'll bring it home for spooky Halloween parties like my daddy does. An' I'll pretend I'm a ghost, an' sneak outa the fog an' yell 'boo' an' scare everybody."

Well, that explained why Alden Crowder had brought dry ice home, but it seemed to Sarah a strange and potentially dangerous Halloween prop.

"Fernie bought his lamp at the mall. At the Barrel of Laughs where they sell the dirty T-shirts." The volume of Bucky's voice was on the rise again.

"Dirty T-shirts?" echoed Sarah, trying to remember if she'd seen any secondhand clothing stores in the mall. She hadn't. "You must be mistaken, Bucky. They wouldn't sell clothing in the mall that isn't new and clean."

"They do too," squealed Beth. "Mummy wouldn't buy us any for Christmas because she says they're pono—porno—"

"*Pornographic*," shouted Bucky. "It means—"

Sarah clamped her hand over his mouth and glanced around to see if anyone had heard. The museum docent had. She pulled the plug on the malfunctioning computer and headed their way. Bucky wiggled free and began to explain the meaning of *pornographic* at the top of his lungs. "*Hot rodders do it four-on-the-floor* is one," said Bucky.

Sarah wasn't sure what that meant.

"Madam," said the docent, "I'm afraid I shall have to ask you and your children to leave the museum."

"Well, I guess that's enough science for today," Sarah mumbled. She glanced at her watch. Two hours to go, and she had yet to find out anything about Maude Crowder's accident. Did the children like her well enough to tell all? Was there any *all* to tell?

"I'm hungry," said Bucky.

"Good, there's a nice salad bar—"

"*Oh, yuck*! shouted Beth. "I hate salads. Daddy calls 'em rabbit food. When I'm a daddy, I'm never gonna eat salads or oatmeal or Brussels sprouts or . . .""

Sarah hustled the two children out of the museum before the docent could summon a security guard.

"Was your father upstairs when your mother fell?" asked Sarah, uncomfortable in her role as undercover interrogator. Perhaps she should read the children their rights, or their father's rights.

"Nope, we were all downstairs playing with the funny ice," Bucky answered.

"Oh yes, the funny ice." Sarah squelched an impulse to explain the chemical composition and properties of dry ice. Too educational an approach might not be conducive to the free flow of information. "Did Mommy play with the funny ice too?"

"Nope, but Daddy fixed an ice bag for her 'cause she had a headache."

"With the funny ice?" Sarah laid her *taco* on the plate. She didn't like *tacos*, especially *tacos* that dripped grease when you picked them up. "He put funny ice in the ice bag?"

"Yep," said Bucky. "With a scoop so it wouldn't burn his fingers. He said it would be real good for Mama's head."

"Did he?" Sarah murmured, considering the possible results of confining dry ice in an ice bag. "Much ice?"

"Full up," said Beth. The little girl had a spattering of *taco* drippings over the legend, *My parents went to Disney World, and all I got was this lousy T-shirt.*

Why would anyone go to Disney World if they weren't taking

their children along? Sarah wondered. "Didn't your mother have medicine for her headaches?"

She threw it away 'cause it made her feel funny," said Bucky. "You shoulda heard her scream 'fore she fell downstairs!" For all his little-boy bravado, he looked anxious. "Do you think she'll be home tomorrow? She's supposed to referee my football game."

Poor child. No one had told him that his mother was in a coma. "I suppose you mean she screamed when she *started* to fall."

"Nope, she screamed *before* she fell," Bucky insisted. "I was in the hall, so I saw her. It was really scary. Her head bumped on the stairs. I'll bet her headache was *awful* after that."

"They won't let us go to see her at the hospital 'cause we're germy," said Beth, beginning to look tearful.

Bucky jumped to his feet and shouted, "Let's go play the video games!"

"Beth, why do you want to be a daddy when you grow up?" Sarah murmured as they followed Bucky to the game room. The question had been nibbling at her.

"'Cause daddies don't fall downstairs an' have to go to scary hospitals where their little girls can't see 'em."

"Oh, my dear." Sarah sighed and looked at her watch. Fifty-nine minutes left before she could take them home. Just as she had suspected, she really wasn't equipped to deal with children.

"She doesn't have anything in the medicine cabinet for headaches but aspirin, which wouldn't make her dizzy." Elena selected a corn chip and dredged up some *guacamole*.

"According to the children, she threw her headache pills away, so Alden either lied about that or didn't know." Sarah stared at her *chili relleno*, disgruntled. Mexican food twice in one day was really too much. On the other hand, it *was* Elena's turn to choose the restaurant, and she hadn't seemed very enthusiastic about French food. "I learned several other odd things about that night. First, Maude screamed *before* she fell, not when she started to fall. Bucky was very clear on that."

"You think Alden pushed her? I wish I could prove it."

"Alden was downstairs with the children. But Bucky went into the hall, heard her scream, and saw the fall—after the scream."

"So what does that mean? She was upstairs by herself, probably not on medication. I've ordered the hospital to run tests for drugs, although it's a little late. Her body has probably metabolized them by now, if there were any."

"The second thing, which is even more peculiar, concerns the ice bag."

"What ice bag?"

"Well, she did have a headache, and Alden fixed her an ice bag, but he put dry ice in it—frozen carbon dioxide."

"So ?"

"It's possible—if the seal were airtight—that the dry ice could have vaporized and blown up the ice bag."

"You mean he was trying to kill her with an ice bag?" asked Elena doubtfully. "That's crazy." Then she remembered the exploding snail. Not that it had done much damage to Angus McGlenlevie, Sarah's ex-husband. A few cuts from flying shell fragments. Grease spots and minor burns from the spattering garlic butter. No more than a man wearing a sweatshirt that said *Poets do it in iambic pentameter* deserved.

"It wouldn't kill her. The explosion, if any, wouldn't produce that kind of force. But it might explain the damage to her hair and to the skin at her hairline." Sarah gave up her polite attempts to eat the *chili relleno*. An ominous burning sensation had begun to blossom in her midriff. "If Maude had the ice bag on her head when it exploded and there were dry ice still unvaporized, which is quite possible, well, dry ice is something you don't touch. He warned the children about that. And putting dry ice in an ice bag is, as I said, a peculiar thing to do."

"If it wouldn't kill her, what was the point?"

"I have no plausible hypothesis to offer—" Sarah frowned as she considered the problem. "—unless he thought the colder the compound, the better for her headache. But if his motives were altruistic, why wouldn't he mention having done it? And why the lie about the medication?"

"I take it back about your not recognizing a clue when you see one, but couldn't you find something more ordinary—like a smoking gun or a five million dollar life insurance policy? Come to think of it, maybe I should check into that."

"Good idea, and in the meantime, and with all due respect to your Hispanic heritage, maybe I should go home and recover from the stress of eating Mexican food—"

"—Which never explodes on your weird ex-husband's plate,"

Elena interjected, grinning.

"—twice in one day," continued Sarah as if she hadn't heard that reference to her one brush with the law, "and being asked to leave the children's science museum by an irate docent."

"You weren't?" Elena started to laugh.

"I was," Sarah assured her grimly.

"Detective Sergeant Elena Jarvis." She flashed her identification for the man at Crowder Chemical Supplies.

"Hank Bristow." He shoved a carton out of the way and shook her hand. "We get visits from OSHA occasionally, but I can't remember the police comin'. What can I do for you?"

"I'm checking out some dry ice Alden Crowder brought home several days ago."

"You mean big Buck? He don't like to be called Alden, which is exactly why I do it." Laughing heartily, Bristow moved a pile of catalogues off a bench so that Elena could sit down, then dropped into his rickety swivel chair.

Elena suppressed a grin, deciding that she *liked* Hank Bristow. "About that dry ice . . ."

"Yeah, sure. I showed him how to operate the dry-ice machine."

"Is the stuff dangerous?"

"Nah, not if you know how to use it."

"And Mr. Crowder—I suppose he knows all about dry ice."

"You're kiddin'! Alden don't know shit about any of our products or services. He just sells whatever Maude an' me give him to sell."

Elena smiled encouragingly. In her experience, the less an investigating officer said, the more information the ordinary citizen volunteered. Criminals were another matter.

"You take the dry ice. I had to tell him not to touch it. Then I told him if his ice chest was airtight—ka-blam! It could blow up his truck."

"That sounds dangerous to me."

"Not really. I was puttin' him on, but ole Alden, he propped that lid up with a stick before he'd put the chest in the truck. Even then he probably shook in his fancy alligator boots all the way home—waitin' for his ice chest to explode." Bristow snickered.

"That's a pretty good joke, Hank," said Elena, thinking of poor Maude Crowder.

"Yeah, Alden's easy to fool—dumb, you know what I mean? If it wasn't for Maude, there wouldn't be a business, an' it's good-bye Crowder's if he gets it in the divorce, but you can't tell him nuthin'. I said to him myself that he'd never be able to run it on his own, but Alden thinks he's hot stuff. Told me just yesterday about all his expansion plans." Bristow snorted. "He ain't got any money to expand with. If Maude don't get outa the hospital quick, we'll be bankrupt."

Elena felt quite pleased with herself. There was a large insurance policy on Maude's life—still in force, with Alden as beneficiary—the expansion money. The fact that the ice bag couldn't actually hurt her was irrelevant. If he *thought* it would, he was guilty of premeditated murder—well, attempted murder. Maude was still alive.

"What do you mean, you got a search warrant?" Alden Crowder blustered. "Search warrant for what?"

Elena doubted that she would find the ice bag in question. Too many days had passed since it blew up on Maude's head, *if* that had actually happened. Even if Elena found it, the D.A. wasn't going to be happy about the prospects of getting a conviction against a husband who gave his wife an exploding ice bag. Not when she'd been injured by a fall, not an explosion. The doctor was pretty clear about the fall. In fact, he'd laughed his head off at the ice-bag theory, although he admitted that it explained the odd skin and hair injuries. Still, having pursued the investigation this far, Elena wanted to know exactly what had happened.

"You just sit right here, Alden," said Elena.

"Buck. Why the hell don't anybody call me Buck?"

"We'll be through in no time." She motioned one of the patrolmen upstairs. The other was to remain behind with Alden.

"Listen, my kids are asleep."

"We may not need to go into their rooms."

"But what are you looking for?" Alden was sweating.

She ignored him and turned over a wastebasket. Then she methodically worked her way through all the other wastebaskets on the first floor. In the kitchen she found what she was looking for—the blue plastic cap, the ring into which it had been screwed, and attached to that, the ragged remnants of the blue pouch. Would dry ice leave traces that could be identified in a lab? Should have asked Sarah. She slid the remains of the attempted murder weapon into a plastic evidence bag, careful to leave intact any fingerprints that might remain.

Sarah and Elena were having dinner before attending the weekly meeting of their support group. "Maude regained consciousness yesterday," said Elena. "She might even be out of the hospital by next week."

"Well, what did she say?" Sarah dipped her salmon *sushi* in the *wasabi* and soy sauce mixture.

"I don't know how you can eat that raw fish. It's probably got all sorts of germs."

"Parasites," said Sarah calmly and picked up a California roll with her chopsticks. Elena was poking suspiciously with her fork at a pile of *sukiyaki*.

"She said the ice bag blew up on her head when she started down the stairs, scared her half to death, and she missed a step and fell. I found the remains of the ice bag among the TV dinner cartons and Twinkie wrappers in the kitchen trash." Elena took a swig of Kirin beer. Not bad for foreign stuff, she decided, but it was the only thing she'd liked so far. "Dumb bastard—first he tries to blow her head off, and he's too stupid to know it isn't going to work. He actually believed the guy at the company who told him dry ice would blow up an ice chest. And then he doesn't even bother to get rid of the weapon."

"Does she know what he did?" Sarah poured *saki* from a delicately glazed porcelain bottle into the matching saki cup.

"I told her. She said, 'That does it. He has to move out.' Which is a big step for Maude. Of course, then I had to tell her he's in jail." Elena held up a cellophane noodle and decided she'd seen things in a bait shop that looked more edible. "Maude said, if he thought she was going to put up bail, he could think again. She's pretty mad."

"And do you have enough evidence to get a conviction on an attempted murder charge?"

"It's about as likely as my chances were of getting you convicted for trying to blow your husband up with a snail." Elena grinned.

Sarah's eyes were twinkling. "My dear Elena, I am not Alden Crowder. If I had wanted to blow Gus up, you can be sure that I'm knowledgeable enough to have done so."

"You're never going to tell me about that, are you?"

"Tell you about what?" asked Sarah, accepting her bowl of green tea ice cream from a bowing waitress in a slightly shabby *kimono*.

"Alden did—he confessed as part of a plea bargain, so I don't need a conviction."

"I'm delighted to hear it," said Sarah. "That should mean that Maude will get Crowder Chemicals." She savored her first spoonful of ice cream. "Aren't you pleased? Justice has triumphed again."

"I suppose," said Elena. But she still wasn't ordering any snails around Sarah Tolland. Come to think of it, she'd keep an eye on anyone offering to fix her an ice bag. Cases like these made you appreciate a good, straight-forward drive-by shooting.

The Big Split

Judith Post

I will never try to convince anyone that I'm a perfect person. My flaws stick out like porcupine quills. I take life too seriously. I take myself too seriously. And my career is almost close to being my religion.

I do have my good points, though. Or at least, my friends assure me I do. Loyalty. Caring. A sense of humor. They tell me that I don't deserve the headaches that Drew is causing me.

Drew and I met when we were both just starting out. He was full of big dreams and I was bristling with ambition. His easy-going charm complemented my lemming-like charge for success. While we were in the first throes of love, I admired his ability to soothe my adrenalin-pumped ferocity. While he struggled as an artist and I strove to climb the corporate ladder, he taught me to stop and smell the roses. He explained that music often charmed the savage beast. When we married, he introduced me to the pleasures of rich food and good wine.

It didn't occur to me for quite some time that all of these domestic extras were being paid for by me, that part of my gut-level panic was the realization that I was sole support of our luxuries and cash flow. It took me even longer to admit to myself that Drew's big dreams were just that. Dreams without discipline die a sure death. It was even harder to survive the slow dissolution of our marriage, the arguments when I suggested that perhaps

Drew should look for a job, the accusations that he'd given me the best years of his life and all I cared about was money. The truth is that money was Drew's big obsession, not mine. Drew was perfectly happy living off of my income with no career of his own. I'd never have been satisfied being a lover and a leech.

Sorry. That sounded bitter, and I guess I am. But I went to see my lawyer yesterday, and the news wasn't good. Our divorce has been pending for a long time now, too long. I wanted it ended. My lawyer assured me that he's done his best. The only big issue was how much I'll have to pay to rid myself of my husband. My lawyer claimed it's going to be plenty.

I drove to my apartment building in a foul mood. Seeing Drew in the lobby did nothing to improve my temperament.

"Don't you ever work?" I asked him. Supposedly, since we'd separated, Drew was actually selling some of his art work. Not very amazing, considering that he was actually painting some pictures to sell. When we'd been together, he'd never picked up his oils or brush. "Or do you spend all your time giving lists of demands to my lawyer and waiting here to harass me?"

Drew gave his crooked smile. In the old days, that smile had melted my heart. Now, it made me want to hit him.

"I've missed you," he said.

An older lady, glancing through a magazine, eyed the two of us appraisingly.

"Me, or my money?" I countered. "No wonder you're asking for such high support payments. It must be expensive living in my lobby."

"It's only fair," Drew said with his usual aplomb. "You raised my standard of living. It's quite heady being married to a brilliant exec. Can I help it if you ruined me for the life of a struggling artist?"

"You bastard!" I hissed. "Quit playing games with me. If you have a problem, call my lawyer."

I turned to walk away, but Drew grabbed my arm. "You could always take me back and avoid all this unpleasantness."

I gaped. Never once had there been any hint of a reconciliation. Things had gotten too unpleasant. "I'd rather die," I said. "Actually, to be honest, I'd rather *you* did."

The older lady looked up, shocked. Rattling her magazine, she crossed the lobby to sit at the far end.

I turned to Drew and glared. "Go away."

"We need to talk in private," he insisted. "I'm tired of all this hostility. It's affecting my work. I'd like to end this thing, one way or another. Our lawyers are making it worse. Can't we just talk?"

I hesitated. I'm used to meeting problems head-on. I was tired of arguing with lawyers, myself.

"Thirty minutes?" he asked. "Can you spare me that?"

I was tired. I was embarrassed, arguing in the lobby. I gave in. "No games," I warned. "Get to the point, then go."

Taking my arm, he led me to the elevator. A couple was loading packages from a shopping expedition into its cramped space.

"Let's take the stairs," he said.

We climbed the first set of steps and reached the landing when Drew suddenly pinned me in his arms and pressed me against the wall. He kissed me passionately. I swear to God, I thought I was going to puke.

"Let me go!" I cried.

"I want you back," Drew told me. "I'll do anything. I'll sell a painting a week. I'll scrub floors, cook gourmet suppers. I'll screw you every night."

I suppose he thought he was being romantic, and that I'd be overcome by passion. Instead, I stomped on his foot with my high-heeled shoe and pushed him away from me with all my strength. Drew fell backwards, grabbing wildly for the railing, but just missing it.

I scrambled down the stairs after him. He'd landed at an odd angle and lay in a heap on the tile floor. No moans, no movement—nothing. Desperately, I felt for a pulse.

Ugly fears enveloped me. We'd been arguing. We were in the middle of a nasty divorce. I'd just come from my lawyer's office, and he'd told me I'd have to make a sizeable settlement.

My mind whirled. Would anyone believe this was an accident?

Stay calm, I told myself. How many times had I been the epitome of cool rationalization in heated business arguments? That's what I was known for. A clear head.

Cold sweat made me shiver. My mind was fevered, but my body was clammy. The more I told myself not to panic, the more I panicked.

I recalled our argument in the lobby. The old lady had moved when I told Drew I'd like to see him dead. If I called the police, what would she tell them? Would anyone believe this was an accident? The term "Reckless Homicide" echoed through my mind.

I glanced at the door that led to the parking garage. Drew's Camaro was parked right next to the building. I walked to the car and opened the back door. I grabbed Drew's shoulders and tried to pull him outside. He was a dead weight. Pushing and shoving, I stuffed him onto the back seat, out of sight, and locked him in.

I couldn't think what to do next. I sat on the bottom step and cried. I know—a real intelligent response, right? But my nerves felt like jangled wires, and I was sure I was going to short-out soon. I was sitting there, watching my life go up in ashes, when Leslie almost tripped over me.

She had her arms full of dirty laundry and she peered at me in surprise. "What the hell do you think you're doing?"

Leslie is my next door neighbor. Without her, I wouldn't have survived this long. She's older and wiser than I am. She's also a great deal more cynical. Perennially single, she's never met a man she could fully like. A thud sounded behind her, and I focused with puffy eyes on Marie. Marie lives across the hall from me. She dresses in ruffles and bows and has devoted her life to being the perfect wife and mother. Talk about two opposites. Yet between the two of them, they've seen me through. They give me a certain sense of balance. Until today, that is.

"Andee! What's the matter?" Marie cried. For only being in her mid-thirties, she has the knack of mothering. She excels at it.

"I just killed Drew," I said.

Instead of going into shock, they sat down beside me, one on each side.

"Of course you did," Marie soothed. "And how did it happen?"

I've heard her talk to her six-year-old in the same rational tone of quiet reason.

When I finished my explanation, Leslie shrugged. "Too bad he died so fast," she said. "The creep deserved to suffer."

"It wasn't your fault, you know," Marie added. "Drew was a truly rotten husband. No woman could possibly put up with someone like that. You didn't mean to kill him."

I could feel myself coming unraveled. It was only a matter of time before I'd be blubbering and pulling out my hair. "But I did kill him!" I yelled. "He's dead, and who's going to believe that it was an accident?"

Leslie frowned. "She's right, Marie. The system always bashes people who kill creeps. They don't want it to catch on."

They stared at each other a moment before Marie said in her pleasant, steady voice, "Then we'll simply have to make sure that she doesn't get caught."

Leslie smiled. "It can't be that hard. No one saw anything, did they?"

I shook my head.

"And you stuffed his body on the back seat?" Leslie persisted.
"Yes."

"Then you and I will drive him home, and Marie will swear that we all did laundry together, won't you, Marie?"

"Of course. There's no reason for Andee to get blamed for something that wasn't her fault. Except that, you might want to disguise yourselves," she suggested. "If anyone notices Andee driving Drew's car, they'll be sure to mention it, when his death is publicized."

Leslie beamed. "Marie, I never realized you were so good in emergencies."

"What do you think having children is all about?" she asked, reasonably.

With that, we went to my apartment and I dressed myself in some of the clothes that Drew had never bothered to take with him. When I was finished, I'd pass a quick inspection—if no one looked too closely. We decided that Leslie would wear a gray wig and a shawl and drive Marie's station wagon. The consensus was that no one would recognize Leslie that way and her car would be in the parking lot the entire time so no one would ever suspect that she'd left. Marie would stay behind, bustling back and forth from the laundry room to her apartment, keeping a highly-visible profile.

When Leslie and I finally left, we were all fairly pleased with ourselves. None of us thought we'd survive long in a life of crime, but we sincerely hoped we'd get lucky enough to slip through this ordeal. My brain was beginning to function once more, and I was beginning to see a ray of light at the end of the tunnel.

Wearing gloves and wiping the car handle clean, I drove Drew's car to his apartment complex. Leslie followed in Marie's station wagon. I parked in one of the front spaces, propped Drew into a sitting position in the back seat and left him there. Then I got in with Leslie and we drove home.

Once Leslie and I were in the basement laundry room with Marie, my knees turned to jelly. My God, what had I done? I'd killed my husband and turned my friends into accessories to the crime.

"We shouldn't have done this," I said.

"Quit fussing," Leslie ordered. "What else was there to do?"

I'm sure there had to be other alternatives, but I couldn't think of any at the moment.

"You're both invited to my apartment for a toast," Leslie said. "I have a bottle of white wine I've been saving for a special occasion."

"A special occasion?" I gasped.

"Drew will never bother you again," Leslie pointed out. "And we accomplished exactly what we set out to do. Surely, that's something to celebrate?"

I had to agree it was. The three of us went to Leslie's and spent the afternoon in fits of gossip to relieve our stress.

All evening long, as I sat in my apartment, I expected the telephone to ring. A subdued voice would say, "Mrs. Bertell, this is Sergeant Jones at the police station, and I'm calling to inform you that your husband was found murdered in the back seat of his car this afternoon." Should I gasp in surprise? I wondered. Should I go into hysterics? I rehearsed it over and over again in my mind, but no one called. How long would it take for someone to notice Drew sitting in the back seat of his car?

When I got to work this morning, I asked my secretary, "Any calls? Anything urgent?"

"Your lawyer phoned," she told me. "He said that everything was finally settled. He made an appointment for you to see him at ten tomorrow morning. Then you're home clear."

I swallowed the fear that had risen like bile in my throat. "At last," I said, trying to sound as relieved as I should have been.

All day passed—and nothing. What if Drew sat in his car for weeks? What if he bloated and started to rot and nobody noticed?

It was almost four-thirty before a policeman knocked on my door. He stuck his head into my office and said, "Mrs. Bertell? I'm Sergeant McCoy. Do you have a minute?"

My palms began to sweat and I wiped them on my skirt as

I rose. "Come on in." Authority has that effect on me. I tried to keep my voice from shaking.

"I'm sorry to have to inform you that we found your husband's body today," he said. "Someone bashed him over the head with a fireplace poker in his apartment. We believe he must have died between nine and ten o'clock last night."

I grasped the edge of my desk, almost losing my balance. The policeman threw out an arm to steady me.

"That's—that's impossible!" I gasped. "I saw Drew yesterday."

"You two were separated, I've been told."

"Yes, our divorce is almost final."

"Do you know if Drew was seeing anyone else? Maybe there was a jealous husband . . . " He let the idea hang between us.

I stared at him blankly. For a supposedly intelligent woman, I didn't seem able to cope, lately. I'd prepared myself for all sorts of business and career emergencies, but I'd never, ever prepared myself for anything as bizarre as all this.

"I'm sorry, ma'am. I can see that you're still shaken up by the news. What if I talk with you again later? You need some time to absorb all of this. Do you have a friend you could call?"

I nodded. "Two of them."

"Why don't you call them now and go home for the day? I'll get in touch with you later."

"Yes, thank you."

As soon as he left, I dialed Leslie's number. "Leslie, you're never going to believe this. Something incredible has happened."

After I told her the news, we agreed that she and Marie and I should meet at my place as soon as I could get home. My secretary was all sympathy and condolences as I prepared to leave. I know I looked the part of the stunned widow.

"Don't you worry about a thing," Margaret assured me. "I'll re-route all your appointments for the rest of the week. Is there anything you need? Anything I can take care of for you?"

Margaret was the best, and I smiled my gratitude. "No thanks, but I appreciate the offer. I'll be all right. I just need some time to think."

Eyes followed me out of the office. I was a miserable picture, indeed.

When I got home, Leslie and Marie hurried to join me.

"Now, tell us everything again, from the beginning," Leslie ordered.

I recited what the policeman had told me.

"Very odd," Marie sighed. "Drew lived in that apartment complex over on State Street, didn't he? Mandarin Courts?"

I nodded.

"I have a friend who lives there. Maybe we should pay her a visit."

"What for?" Leslie asked.

"Sherrie never misses a thing," Marie informed us. "If there's any gossip, she hears it. If there's a scoop, she's on top of it. She makes most reporters look like amateurs."

"That's not such a bad idea," Leslie agreed. "We can use all the inside information we can get. Let's go."

We all bundled into Marie's station wagon and set off. When we reached Mandarin Courts, Marie led us to apartment 3A. At first, I hesitated slightly. Drew had lived next door in 3B. It gave me a squeamish feeling to walk down the same hallway that he must have used the night before. When *what*? Someone dragged his dead body into his apartment and beat him over the head with a fireplace poker? I hunched my shoulders. That didn't make sense. If Marie could help me get to the bottom of this, then I was all for it.

Sherrie Doyle answered the door on the second knock. "Marie!" she crowed. "I haven't seen you for ages. And you brought friends!"

Instead of sounding put-upon, Sherrie sounded delighted. Her bright brown eyes sparkled with curiosity as she surveyed Leslie and me as brand new material for her gossip fodder.

"Sherrie, you won't believe what a coincidence this is," Marie hurriedly explained. "But these are my dear friends, Leslie and Andee. Andee was in the middle of a divorce from your neighbor who got murdered last night."

Sherrie clapped her hands in sheer pleasure. "So *you* were Drew's wife!" she exclaimed.

"Yes." I didn't have to pretend to be completely shaken.

"You really threw him for a loop yesterday," she said with a wink.

"What are you talking about?"

She gave a throaty laugh. "He always bragged that he could wrap you around his little finger. He couldn't believe the way you treated him yesterday."

"*Me*?" I could hardly force the word out.

"Don't play coy with me," Sherrie chuckled. "Drew told me how he made a pass at you and you knocked him down the stairs. The next thing he knows, he comes to with one hell of a headache in the back seat of his car, parked in his own parking lot." She laughed at the monstrosity of the joke. "Believe me, he got the point. If you were that mad, he knew it was over."

Leslie and Marie looked at me. I looked at them. All three of us had assumed he was dead. I'd felt for a pulse. I hadn't found one. Obviously, I wouldn't make much of a nurse.

"That's when he called his lawyer," Sherrie said. "But, I've got to tell you, the man's ego was smarting; he was determined to bleed you dry."

I blinked in astonishment. Drew hadn't been dead when we brought him home, but someone else had killed him. It was too unbelievable!

"You know, Drew told me over and over again that his lawyer, Jim Reyburn, was one of the best in the business. They meant to give it to you good, girl."

"Reyburn!" I shook my head to try and clear it. "Reyburn is *my* lawyer!" I protested.

Sherrie looked at me blankly. "Can't be. I've seen him at Drew's apartment myself. I know his face from his picture in the papers. He's pretty famous, you know."

"I hired him," I reiterated. "He was working for *me*. I have the legal fees to prove it."

"Hmm," Sherrie said, her forehead puckering. "Sounds to me like there's something rotten in Denmark."

It was beginning to sound that way to me, too. After all, for being such a hot shot lawyer, it was Reyburn who kept dragging his feet on the divorce. It was Reyburn who told me I'd have to give blood to get a settlement with Drew. I may not qualify as Ms. Rambo, but when it comes to business, I know a dirty deal when I hear one.

"Lady," Sherrie said sagely, "I think you were being taken to the cleaners!"

When I looked at Leslie and Marie this time, it was with pure fury. "I hate being swindled! What should I do?"

Sherrie's lips twisted into a sweet smile. "Look, honey, I try not to stick my nose into other peoples' business, but I couldn't help overhearing a big argument between Drew and some man last night. I was taking a bath, or I would have gone to the drapes to see who it was. They were out on Drew's balcony, and really going at it. They must have thought I wasn't home, because no lights were on in my livingroom. I don't know if that can help you."

She smiled again. She knew very well what she'd told me was a juicy exclusive. I smiled, too. I intended to use it well.

As we left, Leslie said, "I was just thinking—if a tall, thin, somewhat attractive woman like myself visited a crooked lawyer and claimed to live in 2B, directly beneath Drew, and also claimed that she was occasionally involved with the man, and that she heard Drew and his lawyer argue last night, and then she heard a big crash—do you think that might interest Mr. Reyburn?"

Marie and I couldn't hide our admiration. Not one of us would have ever thought we could be so devious. It was nice to know we had it in us.

"Just remember to be careful. Reyburn killed Drew," Marie pointed out. "He's a dangerous man."

"That's why Andee here is going to call that nice police sergeant and ask him to meet her at Reyburn's address. There's no reason he'd be suspicious. Reyburn's supposed to be her lawyer, so it makes sense for her to want her attorney around when she talks with the police."

"God, you're clever!" I said.

Leslie grinned. "Yes, I am. I'm glad you noticed."

We stopped at a pay phone and I made my call. Luckily, Sergeant McCoy was still on duty. I told him that I was at Mr. Reyburn's office to discuss a few problems concerning my husband's death. With only a little persuasion, the sergeant agreed to meet me at my attorney's office in a few minutes.

Marie had to run two stop signs to get us there in time. Even so, we pulled into the parking lot at the same moment as Sergeant McCoy. I explained my suspicions to him in the elevator on our way up to the sixth floor.

To say that he was happy with me would be telling a lie. As a matter of fact, he was furious. But since he was there, and we were there, he agreed to let us play out our little charade.

I must say that Leslie played her part magnificently. She sashayed into Reyburn's office and lied brilliantly. She'd seen

Reyburn arrive at Drew's apartment complex last night, she insisted. She knew he went up to Drew's apartment. With the windows open, it was easy for her to overhear their argument, and the loud crash that accompanied it. Then she'd watched Reyburn drive away. When she went upstairs to keep her date with Drew, she found him dead.

"And do you really think anyone will believe you?" Reyburn queried, his tone patronizing, to say the least.

Leslie's voice gloated its triumph. "Mrs. Bertell might. Drew told me that you were supposed to be *her* lawyer, too. Am I right?"

A chair scraped back from a desk and a scream shattered the silence. The sergeant rushed into the room, but he needn't have hurried. Leslie, who had taken more self-defense classes than most policewomen, had Reyburn pinned against the wall with his arm twisted behind his back.

A little more than an hour later, over wine in my apartment, Leslie, Marie and I went over the details once again. Reyburn had been quick to confess that he and Drew were planning to trick me into making substantial support payments to my ex, which the two men would then split between themselves. Reyburn claimed he had nothing to do with Drew's death, but the three of us figured that Reyburn must have been furious when he found out Drew had tried for a reconciliation. Before Sergeant McCoy took Reyburn down to the station he assured me that the police had a good case against the crooked lawyer. The case will probably drag out for a while, but at least now I can sit back and relax.

Drew is out of my life forever. I didn't murder him, and my friends are not accomplices to any crime. What we are, in fact, is one magnificent ensemble. We raised our glasses for a final toast, before calling it a night.

"To friendship!" I said.

Our glasses clinked in celebration.

The Seventh Dimension

Edie Ramer

Ghosts do not scream. Ghosts wail, keen, lament, ululate, howl, moan and groan. A scream is a cry of danger, and nothing is dangerous in the sixth dimension. So when Juliane's scream sent the air around me vibrating, I flew from the television room. I flew through walls, I flew through ceilings, I flew through doors.

Earlier, Juliane had drifted upstairs with two of the three young persons who occupied Juliane's house. I had remained downstairs to watch my favorite detection show about the lady novelist who solves murders. Just as I spotted a clue, Juliane's caterwaul summoned me.

Another female scream followed Juliane's. I zipped through the last door in time to see Ben, the brother of the current householder, wave a knife at Tracey, the wife of the current householder. To my alarm, Juliane slipped between them.

"No!" she shouted. "Don't do this."

He was stabbing her. Stabbing them. Tracey and Juliane. Cutting through them with one swoop, the dastard.

"Stop this moment!" I hit him upon the head with my fists and gouged at his eyes with my nails, forgetting the lessons of ninety years of ghostly existence. "You blackguard. You bounder. Stop or I'll make you wish you were born with a tail instead of a penis."

He stopped.

The woman, Tracey, slumped to her bed. Juliane glided back,

unharmed and whole and as lovely as ever.

"Ugh," she said, turning from Tracey.

My darling has an aversion to blood in spite of the fact that this was not the first murder we've witnessed. Or, though we don't speak of it, committed. (Which is, we are positive, why we have been fluttering like dust motes in sunlight for the better part of the century.)

"Elizabeth," she said, floating toward me. "You tried to save me."

"But of course, Juliane. You would do the same for me, wouldn't you?"

"Naturally. I even tried to save this adulterous woman, dearest one."

We both looked upon the dead woman, the blood seeping from the pear-shaped bosom, the still face that uncannily resembled mine. The resemblance had aroused ardor in Juliane's breast, and pangs of jealousy in mine. Juliane, I suspected, harbored a similar jealousy toward Daniel, Tracey's cuckolded husband, a fine, upstanding young man whom (if my nature had been otherwise) I might not have spurned if he had come courting during my earlier time on earth.

Pangs—indeed, thrusts—of jealousy were what had catapulted us into this ungodly position. Oh, if we could only go back and undo that night in the dining room when the devil possessed us and we turned our carving knives on each other until we fell to our deaths over the remains of roast beef and carrots.

A decade later, I had attempted to make a joke out of it. "At least," I said to Juliane, "we could have waited until after dessert. I always did fancy cherry cobbler."

Juliane did have the most unearthly wail. She used it again now.

"What?" I asked, looking around to see if Tracey had manifested into the sixth dimension. This phenomenon had not occurred after the last two murders. But those had resulted from, consecutively, simple robbery and drunkenness, with the victims innocent. This victim had the sin of adultery on her hands. (Also on other parts of her anatomy.) When Tracey's form did not flicker into being, I turned back to Juliane.

"Stop this moment," I ordered.

Sometimes I had to be strict with my darling, a lesson learned too late, as are most. Else they would not be lessons, would they?

She pointed. "Look, Elizabeth. He's wiping his fingerprints from the knife. You know what that means."

I shot her an impatient look. Of course I knew. Wasn't it I who watched the detection shows while she preferred the soap operas? My murders were realistic; hers were committed in designer gowns. (Sometimes it was hard to remember what we did with our days and nights before television—for ghosts, you know, are unable to sleep.)

"Undoubtedly, he will blame it on his brother," I said. "Let Daniel take the fall." (I prided myself on keeping up with the current vernacular.)

"He'll get away with it, too." Juliane put a wail on the end of the sentence. "No one knows Ben and Tracey have been meeting clandestinely. That's why he killed her. She was threatening to tell Daniel about their affair, and he was afraid Daniel would throw him out of his house and his job."

"The barbarian." I glared after Ben as he stepped into the adjoining bathroom to wash the blood from his hands. Dark hair curled down his spine, and I had never admired hirsute men.

Daniel's back, on the other hand, was oh-so-smooth. Sometimes to pass the endless hours I would imagine myself . . . I stiffened my shoulders. "The blackguard should not be allowed to prevail in his villainy."

"No. Poor, dear Tracey." Juliane's moan lasted for a full moment. "But how on heaven or earth can we thwart him?"

As we looked at each other, the water faucet turned off. Ben vaulted back inside the bedroom, scrambling into his shirt and pants and shoes. With one hurried glance at the phosphorous numbers on the bedside clock, he ran into the hall and down the stairway. The front door rattled in its frame.

"Daniel will be home in twenty minutes," I said without thinking. Thank heavens Juliane was too distracted to notice my familiarity with Daniel's homecomings.

"Ben will probably come in five minutes later and pretend he discovered his brother murdering Tracey." Juliane spoke with the authority of more than twenty years of soap opera viewing. "And once Daniel is sentenced, Ben will be left in possession of Daniel's business and Daniel's money."

"We have to stop him," I said.

"We can't, Elizabeth, not without ectoplasm. And you know what happened last time."

I shuddered. That memory was worse than the one that had landed us in our predicament. Our first ten years in the sixth dimension I can only describe as a time of anger and hunger. We were still tied to the bodies we'd lost, the way a worm cut in half is connected to the whole. We wanted life. We wanted love. We wanted to eat and sweat and bleed.

Slowly, so slowly that an ant crawled faster than Father Time ticked his eternal clock, the anger paled and we decided to make the best of it. (Although Juliane never did care for my witticisms about finding the secret of youth. But no one is perfect, and I love her anyway.) I can't remember if we discovered ectoplasm in the 1910's or the 1920's. Anyway, we frightened two sets of Juliane's relatives into fleeing the house. Oh, did we have fun! It was almost as good as being alive. But the ectoplasm always left us tired, fading away somehow. Then the last relatives brought the priest.

He called us demons! As if we weren't perfectly respectable ghosts in our own home.

We outlasted the priest. Barely. We were left wisps of our former selves—ghosts of ghosts. Paler than white carnations and as weak as drunkards in a gin shop. I could feel the nothingness as surely as if I could reach out and touch it, for beyond the frail walls of the sixth dimension was . . . no dimension. Juliane never talked about the decades we languished under the attic eaves with the Christmas decorations from four different families. Not until the sixties did we recover enough to float downstairs, uncertain and shaking. (And you can imagine our shock at what we found!)

We had never resorted to ectoplasm again. Naturally, the life of a ghost grew tedious. But pitiful as it was, it was a life. Of sorts.

"Maybe we could—" I stopped. Juliane was already shaking her head, her brow furrowed, with sadness in her dull eyes that had once sparkled brighter than the Queen's jewels.

"Not without ectoplasm." Juliane reached out to pat my shoulder, her palm passing through my upper torso. "Come, Elizabeth, your show is still on. I'll watch it with you."

I glanced at the clock. Ten minutes to go before Daniel came home, his perfidious brother at his heels. Ten minutes before the lady novelist turned the murderer over to the police. The only things we would be turning would be our backs.

"No!"

"Of course we don't have to watch the show if you'd rather not, Elizabeth. We could watch the traffic from the north window instead. Perhaps there will be an accident."

"No, I won't watch traffic, hoping for an accident. Nor will I stare at moving pictures in a box. I wasn't born for this half-existence. I've stood it, my beloved, for your sake, but there comes a time when a woman has to act on her conscience."

"I *knew* you would leave me some day."

"Darling, it's been ninety-five years."

"Whose fault is that? Who took up the knife? Who drew first blood?"

This was an old argument. "You did," I said.

"I did not! I distinctly remember—"

"You're giving me a headache."

"Ghosts," Juliane said through her teeth, "do not get headaches."

"You cannot stop me, Juliane. I love you, but I've made up my mind."

"I hate it when you say that," Juliane wailed. "You're the most stubborn woman I've known, and why I thought I loved you I will never know."

I swung from her to look upon the murder scene. Tracey was white as myself now, heightening our physical resemblance. The blood left a crimson line across her breast. If I used her finger as pen and her blood as ink, I could write Ben's name across the sheets. Then I thought that my penmanship, even after ninety years of non-use, might not have deteriorated to the present standards.

"I won't help," Juliane said. "I'll be fine by myself. Better. At least I won't be cooped up with my murderer every day for every minute. Don't think I'll miss you, because I won't."

"The sperm!" I exclaimed. "The police are bound to check the sperm and will find out it's not Daniel's." In my delight, I bounced toward Juliane like a child on a trampoline.

She shook her head. "The animal murdered her before they commenced their lovemaking."

"Letters, then. They were lovers, there must be letters."

"Have you forgotten the invention of the telephone?"

My shoulders sagged. Then they straightened. If there was no evidence, I would have to manufacture some. Daniel's freedom from incarceration was up to me.

My road lay before me. It led to the seventh dimension, to nowhere. I closed my eyes and began my journey.

"Ah, no, Elizabeth," Juliane wailed. "Don't leave me."

I shut off her cries, focusing on my toes, my feet, my ankles. I went up my body, anatomical part by anatomical part. It was taking too long, and I had to finish before Daniel and Ben returned. I omitted fingernails as mine were clipped much shorter than the fangs Tracey sported. But I feared leaving out anything else. I had to be perfect: the perfect ghost.

My aura pulsed. I opened my eyes. Yes, it had worked. I was almost flesh. Almost blood. Almost alive. My limbs were rounded and had depth. I cleared my throat, and my voice bounced off the bedroom walls, wonderfully eerie. I wanted to dance, to pirouette as fast as a ballerina on a music box. I felt strong and all-powerful.

"You're going to die." Juliane's voice was a whisper compared to mine.

I swung toward her with the same fury I'd felt ninety years ago. "We are dead," I snapped.

"But our souls are alive. You're killing your soul. Please, come back. There's time yet if you do it right now."

Time. I reached toward Tracey's hand and tugged on the diamond ring. It caught at her knuckle. "Go away, Juliane. I have work to do." Concentrating, I gave the ring a jerk and it pulled free. I slid it on my own ring finger.

"What are you doing?" Juliane asked.

"I'm going to be a ghost." My laughter sounded satanic. "Tracey's ghost."

The garage that a former tenant had built onto the library vibrated with the aid of the mechanical opener. "They're here," Juliane cried. "Oh, I can't watch this. I'm going."

A breeze rippled the air waves and she was gone. I bent down and picked up Tracey's white nightgown. (I felt a pang for its color; I would have liked to go out in a blaze of crimson.)

The downstairs door slammed as I glided into the guest room across the hall. I admired my smooth limbs in the moonlight. Ninety years and as shapely as ever!

"Tracey," Daniel called. "Tracey!"

His footsteps clumped to the kitchen. The refrigerator clicked open. Tracey's nightgown slid over my head. "Perfect," I said to the mirror. (If only Juliane had stayed long enough to see me—I did look lovely.)

My hair wasn't right. I fiddled with it. The telephone across the hall tinged, as if someone were dialing on it. I frowned, then a car pulled up in front and I hurriedly puffed up the sides of my hair. Yes, that was it. I looked enough like Tracey to be . . . her ghost.

"Tracey?" Daniel called from the bottom of the steps. "You taking a bath, Trace?"

The front door opened and shut. "Hi, Dan. Where's Tracey? Don't tell me you two are still fighting."

"What do you mean? We're not fighting."

"C'mon, Tracey told me all about it. Don't bullshit me. I'm your brother."

"I don't know what you're talking about. We're getting along better than ever. What'd she tell you?"

"Hey, nothing. Forget it. I'm sorry I said anything."

"Tracey! What's going on, Trace?" Daniel clambered up the stairs.

I watched from the crack in the door, holding back. It wasn't time yet. And where was Juliane? I thought she would have relented by now. Ninety-five years, and she couldn't even come and kiss me goodbye.

"NO!" Daniel howled.

"What is it?" Ben ran up the stairs.

"She's dead, Tracey's dead. Oh, my God."

"Dan, you didn't." Ben stopped in the hall, his voice stricken. "Did you have to kill her?"

"Call the police. Not this phone, the killer might've used it. Call from the kitchen."

"I'm not calling the cops on my brother, no matter what you did."

"What are you talking about? I didn't kill her. Call the police!"

"It's okay, Dan, don't worry. I'll stand by you. I'll tell the cops we came home together."

"I didn't kill her, I tell you. Now get out of my way."

Daniel stumbled past Ben, lurching down the stairway. The rubber tree in the foyer crashed to the floor. Daniel's fist slammed into the wall, then he stomped on to the kitchen.

In the hall, Ben chuckled softly.

That did it. I was going to scare the sucker into Kingdom Come and back again.

"Oh, Be-e-e-en." I floated through the door, my newly pink limbs glowing under the electric light. "Oh, lover boy."

"Huh?" Ben turned, saw me, backed up. "Oh, no. Oh no, oh no. That's not you. You're dead."

"Yes, little man, I'm dead, but I'm here. Haven't you heard of ghosts?"

His eyes rounded. His mouth twitched. His head shook back and forth. "I don't believe in ghosts. You're not here. Go away."

"If you want me gone, you know what you have to do." As I floated closer to him a siren whined outside, a noise heard more often than birdsong these days. Perhaps there had been an accident on the north road after all.

"Get away from me!" Ben shouted.

I lifted my hands to him, my laughter resonating off the walls. "Darling, from now on I'm going to stick to you like thorns on a rose. The only way you'll be able to get away from me is if you confess."

"Stop! Don't touch me."

"Touch you? Get used to it, dearest. I'll be eating with you, bathing with you, sleeping with you. Won't that be grand?"

There was a pounding on the front door.

Ben looked over his shoulder and back at me. Drool slimed down his chin.

"Police!" a man shouted outside the house. "Open up."

Ben shut his eyes. "You're not real," he whispered. "I'm imagining you. Ghosts don't exist."

"Don't they?" And my Juliane oozed up behind him, her limbs as firm and beautiful and as nearly real as my own. She put her arms around him—those icy, ectoplasmic arms—and squeezed. "Aren't two ghosts better than one?" she cooed into his ear.

Downstairs, Daniel opened the front door. Half-sobbing, he said, "Thank God you came. My wife's been murdered."

In the upper hall, Ben jerked free of Juliane's grasp. Ectoplasm dripped down his neck. He put his hand to his throat and stared in horror from Juliane to me. "No," he said, "I don't believe this."

"Yes," Juliane held out her hand to me, "believe it."

I took her hand and together we advanced toward Ben.

And downstairs someone asked, "Where's the body?"

Ben clutched the bannister, finding the first step with his toe. "Go away," he shouted. "Don't touch me."

Next to the broken rubber tree plant, a man and a woman in blue uniforms turned, their guns in their hands.

"Ben, what is it?" Daniel shouted. "Is the murderer still up there?"

Juliane and I stepped back, out of sight of the officers.

"Can't you see them?" Ben stumbled down the steps, whimpering. "Can't you see Tracey's ghost?"

"Don't do this to me, Ben. Not now."

"I'm not joking. It's her ghost and another one. They're haunting me because I killed her. Do something, Dan. Get them away from me."

"No, Ben, not you, not that."

The woman officer's flat voice cut through Daniel's horror. "Looks like we're going to need the cuffs, Ed."

Hand in hand, Juliane and I floated up to the eaves. I wanted to hug her, but was afraid to take that final ectoplasmic embrace. "You came," I said.

"I couldn't let you go alone."

I stepped back to look once more upon her lovely face, for one last time before . . . "Was it you who called the police?"

She nodded. "Nine-one-one. Our final adventure, my love, although I don't feel at all weakened. Instead I feel as though fireflies have invaded my body."

My skin was itching too, as if it were real skin and not ectoplasm. "Do you see a white light, Juliane?"

"It's in a tunnel. It's beautiful."

The light burned brighter farther down the tunnel, like a thousand suns. Or a thousand souls. Then voices called our names. "Come, Elizabeth. Come, Juliane. Come home." The attic floor became transparent. I could see down into the livingroom, where the woman officer was reading Ben his rights, while her partner handcuffed Ben's wrists together. Daniel was slumped in a chair, his face buried in his hands. In her bedroom, Tracey's body grew colder.

Then I looked back up toward the light, took Juliane's hand, and we stepped into the seventh dimension.

Prosperity Restaurant

S.J. Rozan

The man I'd killed was still haunting me when the new case began. It was two months later, hot steamy summer. The damp Chinatown air was crowded with odors battling like warlords: black bean sauce; vegetables frying in oil; the low-tide reek of fish in boxes of cracked ice on the sidewalk; and the smells of car exhaust and softening asphalt that never go away in summer in New York.

It was a glaring sunny day, and the sidewalks were crowded, half-and-half tourists and Chinese. I threaded my way along Mott Street, past sidewalk vendors selling peaches cheap and the OTB selling luck legally. The jobs I'd worked in the last two months had all been middle-of-the-case lawyer jobs, the kind where the P.I. tails the guy or traces the paper and then reports to the lawyer, collects the fee, and the lawyer settles out of court and the P.I. never finds out what it was even all about.

In my mood, they'd suited me fine; and this one, I assumed, would be the same.

The door to Peter Lee's second floor law office was just past Pale Orchid Imports at the corner of Mott and Pell. Before I went up I stuck my head into the shop to greet Peter's distant uncle, Lee Liang, who owns the shop and the building.

"Ling Wan-ju, how cool and lovely you look!" Smiling, the old man looked up from a packing crate whose contents he was checking. He was speaking Chinese, and he used my Chinese name. It's not what I go by, but I didn't correct him. "How do you manage it in this terrible heat?"

"I don't work as hard as you do, uncle."

"Here, sit. Will you have something to drink? How is your mother, and how are your brothers?"

"My mother is fine, and my brothers are prospering, thank you, uncle. I can't stay; I have an appointment upstairs with Peter." His dark eyes sparkled, and I blushed. "Peter's hiring me for a case."

"If Peter thinks of work when he looks at you, Ling Wan-ju, then Peter is a fool. But," he offered philosophically, "I have other nephews."

"Your uncle thinks you're a fool," I told Peter as I settled stickily in the vinyl chair across the desk from him.

"Uncle Liang? Did he say why?" Peter asked distractedly, shuffling papers. A venerable air conditioner wheezed in the grimy window behind him, trying to convince us that anything working that hard must be making a difference.

"I think because you won't marry me."

He looked up, owl-eyed behind his thick glasses. "Why, Lydia. You never asked me."

"Don't worry, I'm not about to."

Now that Peter's eyes were on me he didn't move them. "How are you doing?" he asked me.

"I'm doing fine," I said impatiently. "How should I be doing?"

Peter shrugged. "Okay," he said. "You don't want to talk about it."

"Oh, for God's sake, Peter. It was two months ago. He shot at me. He had a hostage. It was the only thing I could have done and I'm glad I did it." I didn't add, And he was nineteen. I didn't add, And his shot was wild. I didn't add anything about the shadows in the sleepless nights since then, shadows I search for something to make me believe that shooting a nineteen year old kid through the heart really *was* the only thing I could have done.

What I added, to Peter, was, "Why am I here?"

He settled the papers and leaned forward, resting his weight on his chunky forearms. "Chun-Wei Hsu," he said, "can't find his roommate."

"Who's Chun-Wei Hsu?"

"He's our client."

I shook my head. "He's your client. You're my client. For how long can't he find his roommate?"

Peter frowned at me; then he went on. "Since yesterday."

"Who's the roommate?"

"His cousin. A recent arrival named Li-Han Weng."

"What does he think happened to him?"

"He doesn't know. Li-Han Weng arrived here two weeks ago from Fukien. He's been waiting for his brother, Li-Po, who was supposed to come separately. The brother never arrived and now Li-Han's disappeared."

"One day doesn't make 'disappeared.'"

"Under Li-Han's circumstances, it might."

"What are they?"

"You know Jimmy Tung?"

"Not personally. He owns the Golden Blossom? And Prosperity Restaurant?"

"Here. And two others in Flushing, and one in Brooklyn. A noodle factory in Queens, and a restaurant supply house on the Bowery. He seems to have sponsored the Weng brothers."

"Sponsored." Light dawned. "They're illegals? And Jimmy Tung paid the smuggling fee?"

Peter nodded. "For Li-Han, anyway, and for Chun-Wei Hsu. Chun-Wei says Tung claims he hasn't been contacted about Li-Po's arrival. Li-Han went to work in the factory the day after he landed here."

I got Peter's point. "So you'd expect Li-Han to be trying to be a very good boy so that Jimmy Tung doesn't change his mind about his brother."

"Right. And that doesn't include running off. But . . ."

"But what?" I rearranged myself, pushed my hair back off my face.

"Chun-Wei says he thinks Li-Po did arrive. Chun-Wei works in the kitchen at one of Jimmy Tung's restaurants in Queens. A waiter there told a story about meeting his cousin at the airport off a flight from Taiwan a day or two ago. There was a man who was sick and had to be helped off that flight. The waiter thought there'd be an ambulance and everything, he looked so bad, but two men took him off in a car. Chun-Wei says the waiter's description of the sick man sounded like Li-Po, to him."

"Did he tell this to Li-Han?"

"No, he didn't get the chance."

I thought. "Peter, who are the smugglers?"

"I don't know. Chun-Wei doesn't know. The Wengs had a contact in Fukien and they did what he said. He got them as far as Taiwan, where they separated." He shrugged. "Lydia, Chun-Wei Hsu came to me, but he's really scared. He's afraid for his cousin; he's also afraid he'll lose his job, get found out, get shipped back, screw things up for everyone else from his village who wants to come here. I promised him we'd keep him out of trouble."

I was silent for a minute. "I don't like people making promises for me, Peter."

He spread his hands helplessly. "He was ready to bolt out of here the minute he came in. It was the only way he'd let me help him. If you don't want to take it . . ."

"Oh, of course I'll take it! And of course I'll try to keep him out of it. But I don't like people promising I'll do something I may not be able to do."

Peter looked down at the desk, then back at me. "Chun-Wei says Li-Han was worried; apparently the reason he and Li-Po didn't come together is that Li-Po was sick when Li-Han left Taiwan."

Peter and I listened to the air conditioner try.

"They're from Fukien," I finally said. "Then they're not related to Jimmy Tung."

"Not as far as I know."

I chewed my lower lip. "The going rate for entry to this country," I thought out loud, "is $20,000. Why would you pay that for someone you're not related to?"

Peter grinned a tired grin. "When I see some of the people who come through here," he said, "I sometimes wonder why you'd pay that for people you *are* related to."

So with that and a few others facts filed away, I left. It was early, but I was hungry, and Prosperity Restaurant makes really good pepper shrimp.

The restaurant's old formica tables were about half full, mostly with tourists. In about twenty minutes when the garment sweatshops broke for lunch that would suddenly change. The clack of chopsticks would replace the jingle of forks against plates, and the high-pitched, abrupt voices of the women workers calling to each other and to the waiters would replace the tourist chatter. When the workers' half hour was up it would change back just as fast.

I ordered pickled cabbage soup and pepper shrimp. It's good to eat hot food on a hot day; it makes you sweat. Anyhow, that's what my mother says. I poured sweet, fragrant tea into a thick cup and asked the waiter to point out Jimmy Tung. He said Mr. Tung was not in the restaurant.

In fact, as I dipped the china spoon into the salty soup I noticed there was no one I knew in the restaurant. My brother Elliot's father-in-law worked at Prosperity Restaurant until a year ago, but he and the other organizers had been fired after a failed attempt to unionize. Now all the red-jacketed waiters bustling back and forth around me had unfamiliar faces.

And Fukienese accents.

After lunch I went for a walk. Prosperity Restaurant was on Division Street, a sort of no man's land, but the Golden Blossom—more of a banquet house than a restaurant—was on Mott just off Canal. That made Jimmy Tung's loyalties clear: Mott Street is On Leong tong territory, patrolled by the Ghost Shadows.

Of course, Jimmy Tung might be just an honest businessman who paid his protection money and kept his head down.

On Mott near the corner of Park I found the address Peter had given me for Weng and Hsu. It was an ill-kept five-storey tenement, all age-grimed brick and pigeon-spotted limestone ledges. I pushed open the unlocked outer door.

Inside the narrow vestibule were sixteen mailboxes, some with doors bulging where they'd been pried and badly repaired. A few of them had names on them—Tam, Kwon, Chan—people who could be living here now, or could have lived here before I was born.

I hadn't planned to go inside. I didn't know which apartment Chun-Wei Hsu and his vanished cousin lived in and I probably wouldn't find anything helpful there if I did. I was really just walking and thinking; but as I was thinking the inner door opened and a man stepped into the vestibule. He gave a little start when he saw me, then a shy smile. He held the door and moved aside so I could pass.

I smiled back and said, a little breathlessly, "Can you help me? I'm looking for my cousin, Li-Han Weng, only I don't know which apartment he lives in."

His smile grew a little uncertain, and he shrugged. I repeated the question in Chinese.

This time his face clouded. "I don't know," he said. He turned and hurried out.

I watched him go, then shut the inner door behind me and headed up the stairs. The hallways were dim and peeling, heavy with the smells of peanut oil and nameless funguses. Three rotting oranges lay in a plastic bag at the top of the second floor stairs. I picked a random door on the third floor and knocked.

Behind the door a man's voice rose in complaint and was answered by another. Then footsteps, and the door was opened.

The man who opened it looked tired and short-tempered. Dressed in trousers and white T-shirt, he was barefoot, unshaven, sleep-rumpled. He gave me an impatient grunt which meant the same in English and Chinese.

I chose Chinese. "Excuse me. Does Li-Han Weng live here?"

"No," he snapped. "Wrong place." Like the man I'd spoken with downstairs, he spoke, even in those few words, in the unmistakable cadences of Fukien.

From inside came a muttered obscenity. With a sniggering look at me the man at the door answered it; then he slammed the door, clicked the lock. Before he did, though, I got a glimpse of a fan turning arthritically on the windowsill, blowing a stale breeze over the recumbent forms on the mattresses which crowded the floor of the otherwise unfurnished room.

Back on Mott Street, I slipped into a pagoda-shaped phone booth and called the Golden Blossom.

The woman who answered spoke in Chinese. I pulled out my best Long Island accent —this only works over the phone—and said in English, "Hi! Um, do you speak English?"

"English, yes," she said with an air of distaste I could hear through the receiver.

I took a deep breath and babbled, "Oh, good! Well, my name's Tracie Lane and it's my parents' thirtieth anniversary—thirty, isn't that amazing?—and we all really *love* Chinese food and I was at a party—a whatchamacallit, you know, banquet! at your place a couple of years ago when my friend Janet got married— you know, she's Chinese—anyway, we wanted to set up a thing for Mummy and Daddy—like, I think, fifty people—anyway, can I talk to Mr.—what's his name?—Mr. Tung?"

There was a silence; then, sharply, "Mr. Tung not here."

"Oh. Oh, but when will he be there? I can call him back. You know, because like *I'm* supposed to make all the arrangements. I don't know how it all got to be *my* job, you know? But anyway, what if I call back like at four, you think he'll be there then?"

More silence; then, slowly, "Yes. Mr. Tung here at four."

"Goody. Okay, I'll call then. Sayonara." I hung up, picturing her wrinkling her nose as she put the receiver carefully in its cradle. I hoped there was someone in the office with her she could complain to about me.

I gave the phone another quarter, called another number. "Immigration and Naturalization Service," a woman answered in tones that implied she was going to do her best to make me sorry I'd called.

"Good afternoon," I said diffidently. "I hope you can help me. My aunt just arrived from Canton and she's having problems with her visa. Is there a supervisor there she can speak to who speaks Cantonese?"

"Just a minute," she said huffily. She went away and came back. "You want to speak to Jillian Woo," she said as though I should have known that. "I'll transfer you."

As she was transferring me I hung up, because I didn't want to speak to Jillian Woo.

Then I called Mary Kee. I was surprised to find her in, but then she was always telling me half a cop's work is paperwork.

"Lydia! Hey! How are you? How's your mother?" Her voice, as usual, was straightforward, her words a little fast, but clear. When I'm being me, I have a very slight accent in English; Mary has absolutely none.

"She's well, thanks. How's your family? Your new nephew?" Mary Kee is devoted to her sister's sons.

"God, he is so *adorable*! I wish you could see him! I have about a hundred pictures—"

"Well, you can show them to me. I need to talk to you."

She stopped. "I sort of hoped you were calling just to chat."

"At work? You'd kill me if I did."

"Well, that's true, but I wouldn't have this funny feeling I get every time you want something."

"You mean the funny feeling like the sky's about to fall?"

"That's the one."

"Mary, I don't want you to do anything. It's not really even information, what I want. There's just something I need to know."

Mary hesitated. I waited. A male voice shouted a profanity in the background, answered by another. "Okay," Mary finally said. "When?"

"Now? I'll buy you a cappuccino."

"Okay." She seemed to sigh; I chose to ignore it. "Half an hour, at Reggio's."

I walked up from Chinatown to the Village, through dusty streets reflecting heat back out of concrete and granite. The Chinatown street vendors gave way, as I went west along Canal, to electronics outlets and plastics supply houses. North along Wooster they changed again, to small, specialized, pricey boutiques selling handmade lace, cowboy boots, Japanese art supplies.

I crossed Houston, stopped in a little storefront printer I knew where they made business cards While-U-Wait. I didn't wait, just told them what I wanted, and that I'd be back. A little further north there was another change, as the shops yielded to restaurants and coffee houses. One of these, Reggio's, was where Mary and I usually met, for business or gossip. In Chinatown it would have been instant news if the neighborhood's only resident P.I. were seen having tea with a Fifth Precinct detective, even if they'd known each other since grade school. But north of Canal we were only two Asian women taking a break from a day of doing whatever exotic thing it was that we did.

I got there first. I settled in a wire-frame chair at the only empty outdoor table, ordered an iced Red Zinger, and waited, watching the heat-slowed crowds dawdle along the sidewalks.

Mary arrived just after my tea did, striding along with that don't-mess-with-me cop walk. Wearing jeans, a red T-shirt, and a denim jacket which was heavy for the day but hid the service revolver under her arm, she swivel-hipped her way between the sidewalk tables to get to mine.

"Hi." She plopped into a chair, her long loose braid bouncing behind her. "Jesus, it's hot out. I haven't been out since I got in this morning." She peered at me through her aviator sunglasses. "You look cool," she objected.

"I'm a master of disguise," I admitted modestly.

"You know," Mary said, "I actually was glad to hear from you. In fact, off the record, I'm glad it was business, sort of." She signalled the waiter.

"How come?"

"Well, because I heard you weren't working for a while after what happened."

I sipped my tea, shrugged. "I wasn't. But I am now."

The waiter suddenly appeared, hovering over us. Mary ordered an iced cappuccino. When he was gone she said, "So are you okay?"

"I'm fine."

She looked me over, my black sleeveless shirt and loose cotton pants. "You're not carrying," she said.

I raised my eyebrows. "Maybe it's in my bag."

"You're too smart for that."

"Okay, so I'm not carrying. As a cop aren't you glad?"

Mary ignored that. "You didn't get it back yet?"

"My permit? I got it back. I just . . . I don't need a gun for this case, anyhow."

"You used to argue with me that the whole point was you never knew when you'd need a gun. You sounded like a cowboy. I hated it."

"So you should like me better this way."

"Only if you're doing what you want to do, Lydia. Not if you're just still spooked."

The blood surged hot to my cheeks. "*Spooked*?" I kept my voice to an angry whisper. "Mary, I killed a man! Something happens to your head when you do that—" I stopped as the waiter materialized with Mary's cappuccino. She peeled a straw and stuck it in the cloud of whipped cream on top.

After a minute of silence she said, soothingly, "I know. I'm sorry. I don't know what I'm trying to tell you, even. I'm sure you're safer not carrying, and as a cop I have to approve. I just . . ." she echoed my unfinished phrase of moments before.

We sipped our drinks in silence as the light on the corner

changed and the traffic inched along.

"Okay," Mary said. "Let's talk about what you want that I'm not going to do for you."

I watched a cat slither between the cafe tables. "I'm looking for a missing person," I said.

"Are we looking for him too?"

"No." I shook my head. "He hasn't been gone long enough for you to consider him missing, and besides, he's not officially a person.

"An illegal alien?"

"Uh-huh. And that's the first thing I want, Mary. He's from Fukien, he and his cousin, and his brother was supposed to arrive last week, only we're not sure he ever did."

"Who's we?" she interrupted.

"I'm working for Peter Lee."

Mary gave me a cockeyed, almost wistful grin that spoke volumes.

I grinned back, then said, "So everything on my side is privileged information, although I might be willing to sell some, like where Peter's having dinner, and whether he'd consider dating a cop. Anyway, Mary, listen. Who's smuggling illegals in from Fukien? A lot of them seem to work for Jimmy Tung. Does that mean it's the On Leong, and the Ghost Shadows?" I heard myself drop my voice to say those names, even here, worlds away from Chinatown.

Mary stopped smiling, poked her straw around in her drink. "No," she finally said. "I mean, it's not our department; you need to talk to the INS, really, or the Jade Task Force."

"They wouldn't give me the time of day."

"Probably not." She poked some more. "We've heard rumors. New groups, new gangs. A Taiwanese gang called the White Eagles has been running drugs lately, and possibly illegals, but I couldn't prove that."

"Illegals? Fukienese?"

"We think so, mostly."

"Have they staked out territory? Not in Chinatown, or I'd have run across them."

Mary shook her head. "Flushing. And don't run across them. They're bad people."

"Can you give me a contact?"

"You didn't listen. I said keep away from them." Suddenly she was all cop, cold and commanding.

"Mary, they may have my guys."

"I thought it was one guy."

"And the brother, maybe."

"Well," she said, "if they do you can't do anything for them."

I finished my tea and tried a new path. "The other thing I'm wondering about," I said, "is Asian John Does."

"In the past twenty-four hours?"

"Well, that would be my guy. But I'm thinking in general, the last couple of months."

"I don't know," Mary said. "I'd have to look."

"Could you?"

"I could, if I knew why."

"I don't know," I said frankly. "It's a hunch. I don't know what it means."

I gave her time.

"All right," she finally said. "Call me later. But Lydia, stay out of trouble, okay?"

"I'll try," I promised her. She looked dubious as she slurped up the last of her cappuccino.

"Did you bring the pictures?" I asked.

Mary grinned and reached into her jacket pocket. "You bet I did." She drew out a Kodak envelope and we spent the time until the check came lost in admiration of Mary's extraordinary nephews.

That was the cops; now for the robbers.

I stopped at the quick print place, then went window shopping along Mott Street. It took half an hour, as my shirt slowly plastered itself to my back, before I spotted what I was looking for.

When you want something from a gang member it's always better to approach him when he's alone; but gang members are rarely alone. I also don't know all the Ghost Shadows. They recruit from the high schools and from Hong Kong and there are always new faces. And some of the Ghost Shadows I do know wouldn't talk to me under any circumstances. So I was very pleased to see Henry Kwong shuffling out of the ice cream parlor with a triple-deck cone, and I told him so.

"Pig-nose!" I exclaimed. "What joy!"

Henry's big head jerked around, and his little eyes narrowed almost to non-existence in the folds of his face. He was big for a Chinese, and fat for anyone, and not happy to hear his gang nickname thrown at him by a civilian.

"Well, Charlie Chan!" he sneered. "Find a man yet?"

"You should learn your ethnic history better, Pig-nose," I smiled. "Charlie Chan was a cop. I'm just a clan cousin who needs a favor."

Henry and I are in fact related: his people come from the village in Kwangtung next to the one my people come from, and our great-grandfathers were brothers.

Henry scowled and looked around uncomfortably. It probably wouldn't do his reputation with the gang much good to be seen talking to me; on the other hand, it might, if he could figure out how. But figuring things out gave Henry a headache. Finally he fell back on, "I don't do business with girls," and turned, relieved, to walk away.

I slipped my arm through his, headed up the block with him. Still smiling, I said, "There's a new gang in town, in Flushing. Taiwanese, called the White Eagles. Maybe you've heard of them?"

Henry shook off my arm, planted himself facing me. His belligerent stance was compromised by the ice cream cone he licked before he spoke, but I don't think he noticed. "Who wants to know?"

"I do, Pig-nose. I want to talk to those guys, so you find them for me."

"Oh yeah? You gonna make me?"

Most of the gang members' toughest dialogue is lifted wholesale from Hong Kong martial arts videos. It's exasperating, but it makes it easy to answer.

"Don't be stupid, Pig-nose. This thing is way out of your league. You'd better play ball with me, because if you don't, I won't be responsible for the consequences." I had no idea what that meant, but it was exactly the kind of talk that would impress Henry. Then, in a Hong Kong video gesture, I spun on my heel and walked away.

I went over to the Building Department, on Hudson Street, and did some quick research; then I went home. It was just after three when I turned my key in the four locks on our door, one after the other. "Why carry four keys?" my mother had asked, rhetorically. "This way is just as hard on the thief, easier on us."

"Hi, Ma," I called, coming in. "Any calls?" With my mother, of course, I spoke Chinese.

"No," she answered from the sofa, where she was mending an ancient skirt. "Auntie An-Mei is coming to dinner. I'm making watercress soup. She has pictures of her grandson."

"The soup smells great." I bent and kissed her cheek. "Don't count on me for dinner. I'm working."

My mother sniffed. "Working. With thieves and killers. Even Mary Kee's mother feels sorry for me. Who are you working for, the huge white ogre?"

"No, Ma," I answered from my bedroom, where I peeled off my shirt, stepped out of my pants. "Not Bill. Peter Lee. You ought to be happy with this one, Ma. My client's Chinese. His client's Chinese. Everyone's Chinese. Chinese everywhere, thousands of Chinese, stretching over the horizon, as far as the eye can see—"

"Oh, stop, you silly girl!" she grumbled. "When I see husband for you over the horizon, then I'll be happy."

I deflected the husband talk by picking up the phone. I called Peter.

"News?" he asked.

"Maybe. Do you have a car?"

"No. Do we need one? I could rent one."

"No, it's not worth it. This may not work. If it does, we can take a cab."

"Where?"

"Wherever Jimmy Tung is going."

"What are you doing?"

"Just stirring things up."

"Lydia's Law?"

"What's Lydia's Law?"

"When you don't know what to do, get everybody nervous."

I bit my lip. "God, Peter, is that how I operate?"

"I think so."

"Hmmm. Well, just meet me at that tea shop across the street from the Golden Blossom about four-thirty, okay?" Then, because I was a little upset, I said, to get him nervous, "And Peter, guess who owns the building your client lives in?"

"Who?"

"Jimmy Tung."

Then I climbed into the shower. There, in the resurrecting cool of the water, I thought about what I knew, what I suspected, what I was taking wild guesses at. And I planned what I thought would be the rest of my day.

Before I dressed I called Mary. She wasn't in, but she'd left a message for me with the gum-chewing civilian NYPD employee who answered the squad room phone when the place was empty.

"Says here to tell you yeah, she found what you asked about. It says, 'One, four months ago.' Does that mean anything to you?"

"Yes, thank you. Does it say anything else?"

"'Course not. 'Cause if it did, *I* might find out what's going on around here. You want anything else, or can I get back to work?"

"Is there someplace I can reach Detective Kee?"

"If there is, I don't know about it."

That wasn't as helpful as it might have been. I thought for a few minutes, watching the soft breeze from the fan billow the pale linen curtains my mother had made.

I hauled out the phone book, dialed the Medical Examiner's Office. I got to an Assistant M.E. and introduced myself in clipped tones: "I'm Lydia Chin with *Chung-kuo Shih-pao*"—that's *The China Times*—"and I'm doing a feature on Chinese gang violence. I'm interested in an Asian John Doe you had last March. What can you tell me about that case?"

"Yeah, you know, we're getting a lot of those these days." He had an adenoidal voice and seemed eager to talk; maybe he didn't get much opportunity, where he was. "Not John Does. We always got lots of John Does. But now we're getting all these Orientals. Chinese mostly. What's got into you people? You used to be so quiet, sent your kids to college, never any trouble. And the food, used to be nice, eggrolls, chow mein. Now it's all this hot Szechuan stuff and you're all killing each other. What's the story?"

I thought, And I'll bet the laundry puts too much starch in your underwear, too, these days. Aloud, I said, "That's exactly what I'm trying to find out. What can you tell me?"

"Well, actually, I remember that case. Usually they're identified, y'see, the Chinese, even sometimes only by gang names, but it's something. But this one, no one knew him. Maybe he wasn't Chinese, who knows? It's just the John Does usually are. We kept him around a good long time, finally planted him on Staten Island.

But I don't think he'll do you any good, for your story. Now, if you want to talk violence, I had two in here last month, a gang thing, shot five times each—"

"Why won't the John Doe do me any good?"

He stopped his gleeful description, a little annoyed. "Because no one killed him."

"What do you mean? What did he die of?"

"Pneumonia."

As I dressed and did my hair my mother kept up a running commentary, part gossip, part opinion, part news. She was still talking when I stepped out of my room. She stopped talking suddenly, her mouth open; but she recovered quickly.

"You see, I always say you can make yourself attractive if you make an effort. Why don't you dress like that all the time? You could find a husband, you know, if you put some thought to it. Auntie An-Mei has a nephew—"

"Everyone has a nephew, Ma. The man I'm going to see right now is probably someone's nephew." I glanced in the full-length mirror on the bathroom door. The creamy silk blouse under the lavender suit jacket showed just the right amount of skin—on anyone else it would have been cleavage, but oh well—and the lavender skirt was a half-inch shorter than modesty demanded. I had on gold jewelry and plum lipstick and great big darken-in-the-sun sunglasses. My hair was moussed and brushed like a swirling black storm, and I stood five-foot-three in my two-inch heels.

Altogether, I thought, quite fetching.

I took my briefcase from my closet and loaded it up. "So long, Ma," I said, kissing her. "Give my love to Auntie An-Mei, and don't wait up." I went back down the stairs and out onto the baking streets.

I knocked at the door of the Golden Blossom at four-fifteen. Nothing happened. I knocked again, and then spied a small buzzer on the gilded door frame. I pressed it. A moment later the door was opened by a man in an open-necked white shirt. His face registered surprise; maybe he'd been expecting someone else.

But now he had me.

"I'd like to see Mr. Jimmy Tung, please," I said crisply, in English.

"Not sure he here. I check. You wait here." He started to close the door.

"No, I don't," I said. I shouldered my way smoothly past him. "He's here. Tell him Jillian Woo from the INS is here to see him." I gave him one of my new business cards. He looked at me unsurely and left me alone in the vestibule.

A minute later he was back. "Follow me."

I did follow him, down a hallway that smelled deliciously of slowly roasting pigeon.

At the end of the hallway was a door with a framed crimson scroll embroidered with the ideogram for 'prosperity.' The door stood half-opened; my guide led me to it, pushed it fully open, stood aside to let me pass into the crisp, cool, conditioned air.

Behind an elaborate carved desk—too elaborate for the windowless room—a thin, smiling man was sitting. He was in his fifties, I judged, well-preserved, though his black hair was graying at the temples.

He stood and skirted the desk with his right hand extended. I smiled and we shook.

"Miss Woo, is it?" he said, still smiling. "Please, have a seat. I'm Jimmy Tung. What is it I can do for you?"

I put myself onto a padded cloth-covered office chair and looked around, giving my sunglasses time to lighten, which they never do completely. The rest of the room, disarrayed, with old-looking stacks of papers and files on the furniture and the floor, did not live up to the desk.

"Mr. Tung," I finally smiled at the thin man, who'd gone back behind his desk and sat looking pleasantly expectant, his fingers lightly bouncing against each other as his hands formed a little tent over the mess on his desk. "It's a pleasure to meet you at last."

He started to say something and I cut him off. "Of course, I know what you're thinking. Why is the INS here? You thought we had an arrangement."

"I—" His face was innocent surprise.

"Not you, of course, and not me. But you must wonder what good your membership in the tong is doing you, if despite it you're forced to entertain an INS agent in the middle of the day in your own restaurant. The tong is supposed to take care of this sort of thing for you."

"Miss Woo—"

"Ms. And we do have an arrangement, Mr. Tung. It's just not exactly what you think."

I paused a minute, fingering the gold chain at my throat, to let him worry. His eyes flashed to the jade dangling where the cleavage should have been. I went on.

"You employ illegal aliens in your restaurants and factory, Mr. Tung. You do this because you can pay them very much less than actual citizens, who believe they have rights, even in Chinatown. There's always been a certain amount of this scummy business in Chinatown, but all you restaurant owners expanded your scope quite a bit after the Hotel and Restaurant Employees' Union almost got their hooks into your places last year."

I shifted in my seat, re-crossing my stockinged legs; I didn't stop talking. "But you yourself have actually gone beyond the usual practice, in quite an entrepreneurial stretch. You not only employ illegals, you import them. You house them, too, sleeping in shifts six to a sordid room in stinking buildings you own. So out of the very, very low wages you pay these men, they pay you rent, and they repay the smuggling fee you paid—possibly with interest, am I right?—or you threaten to expose them to me and my staff. Very enterprising, Mr. Tung."

"Ms. Woo—" Tung started to protest. The phone on his desk rang sharply. Tung jumped. I looked away, annoyed. Tung gave me an apologetic smile, said, "Excuse me," and picked up the receiver. "Yes," he said in Chinese, then, "Yes, put him through." He smiled at me again, said, "This will only take a moment." After a short pause he said into the receiver, "Mr. Han. I hope you have good news for me?" He listened, and I twirled the jade pendant. "I understand that, and I understand the price is good. But I don't want them." More listening; then, with the sound of an interruption, "Mr. Han, *my* customers *will* notice shoddy merchandise. If you can't deliver the quality you promised I'll buy my linens from someone else." Pause. "I don't care what you do with them. They're nothing I can use and I won't pay for them." Pause. "No." Pause. "Yes." More pauses. Other words, which I didn't hear. I'd gotten it. It had come slamming into me like a missile with an information warhead. I didn't need Peter to meet me later. I didn't need the White Eagles. I didn't need to follow Jimmy Tung, didn't need anything from him except for him to stay on the phone long enough for me to formulate a whole new plan for the rest of our conversation.

And bless his larcenous heart, he did.

When he finally hung up, the argument over, he smiled at me again. He seemed more at ease, a condition I was determined wouldn't last.

"I'm sorry," he said. "What were we—"

"Indentured servitude," I said. "Slavery, almost. We were talking about that. We were talking about why the INS lets you get away with it. You think it's because certain people on my staff are paid off by your tong. Some of the people on my staff think so too, by the way. But that's not it, Mr. Tung.

"What it is is this: there are certain Chinese who, for political reasons, the American government prefers to see out of China. Pro-democracy students and intellectuals, and others. We can't bring them out directly. But we can help them get to Good Samaritans like you." Tung's face was sort of collapsing, like a house built over a sinkhole. "Now, normally we don't interfere. We haven't yet. These men are actually safer for the time being living in your hovels and working in your salt mines than they would be anywhere else.

"But occasionally you reject someone, a faulty import, a piece of merchandise that isn't up to your low but firm standards. Like your linens, Mr. Tung." I smiled very, very sweetly. "In March you rejected a man who was ill, with pneumonia. He died." In the air-conditioned coolness beads of perspiration sprang up on Tung's upper lip. Bingo, Lydia.

"And now we come to why I'm here, Mr. Tung. You've rejected another faulty import, a man known to you as Li-Po Weng. You bought and paid for another man whom you believe to be his brother, Li-Han, but Li-Po is ill. Now Li-Han has disappeared. I think I know what's happened to him."

"Miss Woo—*Ms*. Woo, I don't really—" Tung began.

"Oh, spare me." I stood, no longer smiling. "You didn't pay for the man who died last March. That must have angered the White Eagles, your import agents, right? They let it pass, and you kept doing business together. But when you wouldn't pay for Li-Po Weng, they snatched Li-Han back. Now you're out the brother you paid for unless you pay for the one you don't want."

I leaned on my fists on the uneven layer of papers on his desk. "But the point is, Mr. Tung, *we* want him. We want both of them.

So pay the fee, buddy boy. Get those men here, and get Li-Po a doctor if that's what he needs, because I'm telling you now that the continuing health of your operation depends on the continuing health of the Wengs."

With a broad smile I picked up my briefcase and turned to depart. Tung, white and wide-eyed, said nothing. With my hand on the coolness of the doorknob I looked over my shoulder. "Do it; but don't tell me about it. I haven't been here. If you so much as call my office, I will deny ever having met you." Leaving the door open behind me, I strode down the hallway and into the heat of the late afternoon.

I was sauntering down Mott grinning to myself when I felt someone jostle me, passing too close. I turned my head to snap at him; as I did an arm snaked around my shoulders from the other side. A voice said, "Act glad to see me or I'll shoot you right here." I beamed up into the hard face next to mine and, still smiling, said, "Who the hell are you?"

From the other side of me a different voice said, "Walk, smile, and shut up."

I did those things, noticing as I was hustled into a waiting Jeep Cherokee the blobby form of Henry Kwong standing in the shadow of a doorway across the street. Pig-nose, you little bastard, I thought. These are White Eagles, and you're a stool pigeon.

One of my handlers, the hard-faced one, got in the front, and the other got in the back with me. There was already a driver, who roared the Jeep hard away from the curb. He rocked that big car in and out of traffic as though it were a Porsche, barreling down Mott, around Chatham Square, and out over the Manhattan Bridge.

"Tell me what the hell is going on!" I demanded, but only once, because the kid beside me pulled out a small automatic with a big silencer on it and said, "No." Then he said, "Take your jacket off." I did, handed it to him. He went through the pockets, finding nothing. He tossed it on the floor, reached over and frisked me. He found more nothing.

"Your ugly cousin said you'd be armed," he told me.

"He makes things up."

"Pull up your skirt," he ordered. I felt myself flush a fierce crimson, but I did it. When he was satisfied there was no pearl-handled .22 strapped to my thigh he grinned, lowered the automatic, and slid himself closer to me. I'd lowered my skirt when he lowered the gun, but he put his empty hand on my knee, started to slither up my thigh.

I slapped him, open-hand but hard. He yelped, pulled back, anger reddening his cheeks; then he hauled back and smacked me across the face.

I went with the blow, didn't block it and didn't respond. I couldn't win, here, with the three of them and silenced guns; there was no point in letting them see what I could do and what I couldn't. The sting of his hand made my eyes tear. I yanked myself back against the car door, as far away from him as I could get, and wiped them quickly. I glared at him, fury and contempt equally mixed.

From the front, from the driver, came the command, "Lay off her, Roach. You want that, talk to Ho-kin later."

So I watched out the window from my side and he watched me from his as we sped along the BQE to the Long Island Expressway and then north on a little piece of the Van Wyck. They hadn't made any effort to keep me from seeing where we were going, which I thought was a bad sign.

In Flushing we went a short distance along Main Street, then pulled onto Simpson. The Jeep screeched to a halt in front of the Jade Palace, a strictly take-out Chinese restaurant on the ground floor of a three-storey mint-green aluminum-sided building. People on the street studiously looked in every other direction they could look in as I was hurried, tripping in the damn high heels, in the street door beside the restaurant and up the wooden stairs. The Jeep screeched off, my lavender jacket on the floor of the back seat.

At the top of the stairs Roach pushed open a door and shoved me inside. I kicked my shoes off as I stumbled in. Roach closed the door behind him and leaned on it. I smiled at him. It was like smiling at the wall. Missed your chance with this one, Lydia, I thought. I shrugged, walked around the room.

It was a kitchen. It held yellow cabinets, a yellow formica-topped metal legged table, and cheap metal chairs. The linoleum floor was sticky under my stockinged feet.

"Nice place," I said. "Yours?"

"Keep away from the windows. Sit down, over there."

Moving back toward the table, I pointed to a closed door

leading off the kitchen. "Is that where you keep the guys you bring in until someone pays for them?"

He sneered. "There's no one here but you, so stop hoping. Sit down and shut up." He waved the automatic around. I sat down and shut up.

We were like that for awhile, maybe ten minutes, before there was a coded knock on the door and Roach let Hard-face in, with another man. Hard-face took a position by the window.

The other man looked at me, unsmiling. His face was lined and his nose was crooked, with a scar where the bend was. He was not old, though older than I: thirty-five, maybe. But his eyes held an ancient, unblinking stare which made me shiver in the heat.

Roach handed the new man my briefcase. He opened it, glanced through the old files and junk I'd stuck in it. Then, unhurried, he went to the old refrigerator, took out a can of Miller beer.

In heavily-accented English, he said, "You want me. You find me. Happy now?"

"You're— " my voice, to my surprise, was weak; I swallowed, made my heart slow down, and tried again. "You're the White Eagles' dai-lo?"

"Gua Ho-kin. *You*"—he pointed the beer can at me—"are nosy, stupid bitch. Why you want to see me? Why you go to see Jimmy Tung?"

Thinking furiously, I said, "Jimmy Tung? What does—I'm trying to build up my security business, and I'm looking for clients. Alarm systems, that kind of thing. It's part of what I do. And you, I wanted to see you because I don't like people operating in my territory if I haven't met them."

"Your territory?" Settling in a chair, he seemed faintly surprised and amused.

"Chinatown. It's my home, Mr. Gua. To you it's a prize to be divided up, but I see it a little differently. I have a long-term interest there. You have your operations, as do others, and I know my place, but I also have systems I've developed. If I can help you, or you can help me, I like to know about that." This was complete gobbledygook, but I was hoping his English was weak enough that I could dazzle him with it.

"Tell me," he said with a slow, nasty smile, "why you try to build up security business in name of Jillian Woo. Jillian Woo," he said, taking a handful of my new business cards out of my briefcase and tossing them onto the table, "from INS."

"I—"

"Stop," he said. "Don't lie to me. You lie to me, I cut your face up." Gua reached behind him, fumbled open a drawer, pulled out a big, triangular-bladed knife. It glinted once in the late-day sun. My eyes fixed on that glint, on that blade, and wouldn't let go. I tried to think, but my mind was suddenly spinning free, like wheels on ice, moving at high speed, grabbing onto nothing.

Then a shout from Hard-face, standing by the window. A word I didn't catch; then Gua sprang to his feet, and all three of them ran to the window. Sirens pierced through to my brain, and a woman's voice through a police bullhorn.

Gua shouted an order in Chinese, and Roach spun around to find me, but I was ready. I heaved a chair into the side of his head, dove for the gun as he swayed and fell.

"Gua Ho-kin!" I shouted. Gua stopped dead, arms half-risen from his sides like the wings of a ponderous bird. His cold, ancient eyes were narrowed and fixed on mine. I didn't try to get up off the floor; I held the automatic in both hands. The gun was enormous, unbelievably heavy, hot against my palms. "I'll blow your head off. I know how. I've done it. Don't move and tell him not to move." I said it in Chinese, and was smothered with a sudden wave of fear that my dialect and his were so different that he hadn't understood me. But Gua signaled Hard-face—Roach was motionless on the floor—and the two of them stood still, eyes on me, as I rose.

I hoped they wouldn't see my hands trembling with the effort of holding this heavy, heavy gun. I backed to the window, motioning them away from it. I half-leaned out, yelled, "Come up!" and waited. In seconds I heard the downstairs door being kicked in, and feet pounding the stairs. The room door crashed open and three cops charged in, taking combat positions, guns trained on all of us.

"It's okay," I said calmly, while my heart chattered in my chest. "I'm with you guys." I lifted my hands, held the gun by the grip, offered it to them.

A blue-denim form rose from one knee and said, "That's right, she is." It was Mary. She tucked her gun away, came and took mine. I was glad when it was gone. Mary looked into my eyes; then she hugged me. That was good, warm and reassuring, and I wondered when this hundred-degree day had suddenly turned cold right where I was.

"Are you okay?" Mary asked.

I nodded and tried to swallow in my dry throat. "Just scared."

"Well, it serves you right. I told you to keep away from these guys."

"They picked me up," I protested. "They *kidnapped* me."

"All on their own? What a coincidence."

Gua started to snarl something. The cop handcuffing him shut him up with a word.

Mary took me down the stairs. I asked, "How did you know I was here?"

"Peter Lee."

"Peter?" We came out into the late-day sun. I was about to ask how Peter had any idea where I was, but Peter himself came sprinting across the street. He grabbed my shoulders and searched my face.

"Lydia? Are you okay?" He didn't give me a chance to answer, just squeezed me hard against him.

"Go on over to the cars. Wait for me there." Mary turned back into the mint-green house.

"Peter, how did you know where I was?" He had his arm around me as we walked across the street to the police cars. I tiptoed in my bare feet over the hot, pebbly asphalt.

"I followed you."

"You *followed* me?"

"Well, you told me to meet you at the Golden Blossom. I was on my way there and I saw you with those guys. You didn't look as though you liked them. And you were supposed to meet me but you got in that Jeep. I didn't like it. So I jumped in a cab and followed you."

"The cab driver must have liked that." We sat down together on the thin strip of grass between the sidewalk and the curb. Across the street two uniformed cops were bringing Gua and Roach and Hard-face out of the house in handcuffs. Roach was staggering a little.

"He thought it was great," Peter told me. "He was Jamaican. He kept shaking his head and chuckling and saying, 'Just like the movies, man, just like the movies.' I had to keep telling him not to follow too close." Peter took off his glasses, ran his hand over his face, resettled them.

I kissed him. He blushed, grinned, and looked away.

"How did Mary get here?" I asked.

"After I called 911, I called the Fifth Precinct. I'm not sure why, except I think I thought it was Chinatown crime, it was my fault, I wanted someone there I knew, you know? I was pretty upset by then. I wasn't really thinking."

"First, it's absolutely not your fault. Second, you have great instincts, for a guy with a desk job. Third, Mary thinks you don't know she's alive."

He blushed again. "I didn't think she thought about me enough to think whether I knew she was alive or not."

"Peter, for a lawyer, that's very badly put. *I* think—" I stopped telling him what I thought, because Mary came striding out of the mint-green house, her braid swinging. She crossed the street to her unmarked car, took out its radio mouthpiece and spoke into it. Then she came over to where we were, crouched next to me.

"Found your boys upstairs," she said. "They're both alive, but one's sick and one's hurt."

"Your boys?" Peter asked a little blankly. "The Wengs?"

Mary nodded. "I called for a bus—an ambulance, I mean. One of them's just been knocked around a little, but the other one—the younger one—I think he was telling me he has TB. But my Chinese isn't so hot, so maybe I didn't get it right."

"No, that's probably right. That would explain it. You don't want that in your kitchen," I said.

"What are you talking about?" Peter asked. "Did you know they were here?"

"I hoped."

As Mary started to say something a blue BMW turned into Simpson Street, then stopped, then violently backed out around the corner and sped away.

"Jimmy Tung!" I yelled. "Goddammit, that's Jimmy Tung! I was right! Mary, you've got to—! This is all his—!" Tripping over my words, I looked helplessly at Peter, then at Mary. They looked at each other.

"Okay," Mary said. "Calm down. Explain it to me, and if he needs to be taken up, we'll find him."

So sitting in the long yellow rays of the afternoon sun I explained it to Mary, and Peter. When I was through they both gave me hell for taking chances, charging right in, acting alone on my own wild hunches.

"Hey!" I said. "Hey, you guys! You both saved my life. Thanks. I'm glad. I love you. Now stop. Leave me alone." I stood and walked away, leaving them together on the soft grass. My head was filled with noise, with voices and the smell of rotting oranges and sleeping men crowded together in airless rooms. The ancient cruel eyes of a man not that much older than I was faded into the eyes of a nineteen year old kid who wouldn't get older. I didn't know where I was going, barefoot and rumpled in the heat of the evening, but it was time to be by myself for awhile.

Mrs. Dunlop's New Hat

Caroline Stafford

It all started with my new hat.

I can remember when no self-respecting woman went anywhere without one. Times have changed, of course, but there's still nothing like a nice hat to make you feel all dressed up.

Not that I have many places to wear mine. Merton is just a little Blue Ridge town along one of the old roads that used to wind its way down to Charlottesville in one direction and Waynesboro in the other. We never have much to do with either of them if we can help it. Charlottesville has the university and Waynesboro is full of people who came down to make money in the big plant there. We're mostly farming folk around Merton, and proud of it.

The biggest still busted in Virginia during Prohibition was here in Merton, and during the War Between the States, a Yankee officer was shot by Mrs. Clegg's great-grandmother's sister—then he came back after the war to marry her. And once we had a famous bank robber living here, only nobody knew it at the time. It was his sister's death that started me on my present career in solving crimes.

Which doesn't keep me all that busy in Merton. We've got a gas station and a general store with a branch of the bank next to the dry goods, and a post office around the corner. The beauty shop is in Mrs. Harrison's house and the Misses Dalton keep a notion shop and some potted flowers for sale in the room built onto their front porch. Then there's the Dew Drop Inn, where we get hunters and any tourists passing through around lunch time. The price is right, and you can't miss the Inn if you tried, once you've found your way to Merton. There are only three eating places in town, anyway. Fred's, to one side of the gas station, where you can buy sandwiches and crackers and candy bars, and the men stand around to talk. The Hut, which is sort of the teenage hangout, ice cream and such. And the Inn. Mrs. Clegg owns that, and she's made it right pretty inside, blue-checked table cloths and chintz curtains and a big Welsh dresser full of old plates and pitchers. If I'm tired of sitting at home and feel like going out for a bite of lunch or maybe a piece of pie, I go there. So when I bought a new hat, that was the first place I wore it.

And there I sat, where everybody could see me as they came in the door. Across by the big front window there was this other woman wearing a hat, too. She was not more than thirty, and the nice black suit she had on looked sort of businesslike, with a pearl pin on the lapel. A travelling salesman, I decided. Her hat was more like a man's black felt, but it had a light blue band and a bit of a feather on the side. Mine had a pheasant's feather too, but the hat was gray like my coat and the feather was in the back.

She was watching the road outside, not paying much attention to the other customers. The Inn had been busy for a Wednesday, and in spite of old Miss Davenport in her ratty fake fur, our hats gave the place a nice, respectable air.

When I finished my coconut cream pie and was ready to leave, I got up and went across to the newcomer and said, "That's a mighty pretty hat you've got on."

She looked startled, as if she wasn't used to having strangers speak to her, but people are friendly in the South and don't mean anything by it. "Thank you." She hesitated.

I stood there beside the table, waiting for her to say something about my hat in return, like, "I've been admiring yours, too."

But she didn't. She asked, "Er . . . can you tell me how to get to Covington from here?"

I thought about that, then answered, "Well, it's best to go over to Route 29 first, and head south from there. The old road from here is too hard to follow if you don't know it."

She frowned, still looking at me in that funny way as if she couldn't quite decide what to make of me. I thought maybe she'd seen my picture in the paper and was too shy to say so.

"South from Charlottesville, I mean," I added, in case she didn't know you went east before you turned south. "That's where you pick up Route 29, in Charlottesville. It's marked."

Her face cleared. "Thanks." She got up, leaving the magazine she'd been reading sitting there on the table by her coffee cup. I picked it up and held it out, but she shook her head. "No, no, you can have it. I've read it."

Then she paid her bill in a hurry and was gone. I put the magazine in my carry-all, still put out that she hadn't noticed my hat. But Mrs. Clegg was saying, "Funny—she's heading the wrong way, back towards Waynesboro, not to Charlottesville."

I looked out the window, and sure enough she was going in the wrong direction. "Well, I told her the best I could," I answered. "Maybe she's not going to Covington today." And I paid my own bill, then said good-bye.

It wasn't until I'd gotten home and finished my ironing that I took out the magazine to look at. One of those with tall skinny models in clothes nobody else would walk down the street in, yellow and purple and peacock blue, skirts short enough to give you pneumonia and shoulders wide enough to give you trouble going through some doors. My late husband used to say that designers were out to impress each other, and this year they must have succeeded right well if this magazine was anything to go by. I liked the ads all the same, perfume and make-up and jewelry, so I was turning the pages to see them.

And then something fell out, a long flat bit of funny white stuff.

Now I may live in Merton, but I'm no fool. I see the television like everybody else, and I know all about this plastic bomb that they put in radios to blow up planes and cars.

I stared down at the thing on my carpet and thought, "My time's come!"

But then nothing happened, and I remembered that you have to put something in the middle of this kind of explosive before it will go off. A cap, they call it.

When I'd gotten over my scare, I reached down and picked up the sheet and looked at it. Just flat and soft and grainy and limp, like a thin piece of sponge, only not so full of holes or as squeezy. And it didn't look like it could stand up to much scrubbing. I sniffed it but it didn't smell like much of anything except for the Wild Joy perfume sample two pages back in the magazine.

Now who on earth would want plastic bombs around here? I wondered. And where were they going to be using it? Or were they just passing through like a regular tourist, on their way to somewhere else?

That's when I got scared for a second time. Anybody carrying this stuff around is going to want it back if they lose it, and when that woman remembers I've got her bomb as well as her magazine, she'll be after me!

I thought of calling Howie Jameson, our police chief, but he's an old fool. He wouldn't know plastic explosives if they walked in the door and I couldn't count on him doing anything but making things worse. He usually did.

So I needed to find out what was going on here before I got myself murdered in my bed.

Naomi, my neighbor, called to me as I left the house again to go hurrying back to the Dew Drop Inn, but I told her I didn't have time to talk just then. I had decided to put the magazine back on the chair where the woman had been sitting, as if I'd never touched it—and then watch and see what happened when she came back.

But there was trouble at the Inn already.

A man was there, giving Betty Jo a hard time. Now Betty Jo is Merton's only yuppie. She's marrying a boy going to college down in Charlottesville, and she works in a bank down there. She'd come home to see her mother and was wearing a new corduroy jacket over tweed pants, with a big black bow on the back of her head like some of those styles I'd seen in the magazine.

The man was standing over her and demanding, "Where is it?"

She was looking scared, clutching her Dr. Pepper and saying, "I don't know what—"

The place was empty except for him and her, and Mrs. Clegg over behind the counter. And me, just coming through the door. I couldn't believe my eyes when he hauled off and slapped Betty Jo, right across her face. "You got your money," he shouted. "Now you've got cold feet! Well, you're going to regret it."

"Here— !" Mrs. Clegg exclaimed, coming around the counter. "None of that!"

Betty Jo began to cry. The man glared at all of us and stomped out, pushing past me and slamming the door hard.

I stood there, my back pressed up against the front window and my mind running a mile a minute. That man had looked just like a criminal to me—ugly and mad. Was he planning to rob Betty Jo's bank? Had he somehow tricked her into helping him? Was that what he meant about cold feet?

Betty Jo was still crying. I walked over to her and scolded, "What's your mother going to say when she finds out you're carrying on with a man like that!"

"I've never seen him before," the girl wailed.

"Well, he seems to know *you*," I said.

Mrs. Clegg was patting Betty Jo's shoulder. "Now, now. That's enough." I wasn't sure whether she was talking to Betty Jo or to me or both of us. "Betty Jo? He didn't hit you that hard. Look up here, let me see your face—"

Betty Jo looked up. There was a red mark on her cheek. "He said he liked my hat," she told us in a quavery voice, ready to wail again.

"What hat?" I demanded.

She picked up the big black velvet bow that had fallen off when the man hit her, and clapped it back on the top of her head. It sort of looked like a hat, if you were a man and didn't know better. "I said it was really a bow, but thanked him anyway." Tears started to run down her cheeks again. "And he didn't seem to like that."

"What did he say?"

"Nothing at first. He just stood there waiting. Then he said, as if he was impatient, 'Don't you need some directions?'"

"Directions?" I repeated. Betty Jo has lived here all her life.

She nodded, miserable and feeling sorry for herself still. I was starting to feel scared. Again.

"Directions?" I asked a second time. "Where to?"

"To—to Covington."

"Oh my dear." I sat down at the table, my mind on that magazine and how I'd gotten it. After I'd complimented that woman on her hat, she'd asked me directions to Covington—and now this man had expected Betty Jo, with her funny bow, to ask him the same question. Somehow I'd said the right thing to the wrong person and got myself in the middle of a real fix, because *she* thought I was the one she was to meet here, and now this man had come looking for *her*. But she'd gone.

Terrorists, right here in Merton! One to bring in the bomb and the other to use it. And I'd seen them both. But why would they want to blow up Betty Jo's bank?

Or did they?

It was just like a spy novel, I thought. A real live spy novel. Excited now, I exclaimed, "It's a conspiracy!"

Mrs. Clegg turned and looked at me. "You need a cup of tea, Mrs. Dunlop," she said, and walked off to get two cups and a pot.

I paid no attention, and turned back to Betty Jo. "It's true? You never saw him before?"

"No. Never."

"What're you doing home today? It's a weekday."

"I had the afternoon off. I wanted Ma to see what I was wearing tomorrow when the President comes—"

The President! I'd all but forgotten he was coming to speak at Charlottesville. That's who the terrorists were after! Not Betty Jo's bank, for goodness sake.

"Call the police," I told Mrs. Clegg as she came back with the tea. I was already out of my chair, heading for the door to lock it.

"What's going on?" she asked suspiciously.

But I was too late. Before I could get there, the man came back, this time accompanied by a friend even uglier and madder than he was. They made straight for Betty Jo, shoving me aside like a sack of Granny Smith apples. Mrs. Clegg had disappeared into the kitchen, tea, tray and all.

"Hand it over," the first man ordered. "Or Cleavor, here, will see that you're sorry!"

"Morgan's right," Cleaver rumbled. "*Very* sorry!"

Betty Jo was crying again. I ask you, what kind of woman is that, when the President's life is at stake? Weeping all over the place like an old sink!

"Leave her be!" I said, swinging my handbag into the small of Cleavor's back as he lifted a fist the size of a ham. He growled and turned on me, eyes blazing. I paid no heed. "She's not the one you want, anyway. *I'm* the one with the hat."

Morgan turned, too, and looked at me. Looked straight at my head. That's when I remembered I'd been in such a hurry to get rid of the magazine that I'd forgotten to put my new hat back on.

"You're crazy, old woman," he said, while Cleavor, paying no more attention to us, reached out for Betty Jo. And there was nobody to save her but me. I picked up the Dr. Pepper bottle from her table and swung it hard, hitting Cleavor on the head with a crack that made his knees buckle.

As he sprawled flat on the floor, Morgan lunged for me. I know when to be brave and when to be a coward. I ran. Betty Jo was screaming, Mrs. Clegg's cook had come in from the back kitchen and was yelling, but I was breathing too fast to add to the uproar. There was a big fern hanging from a rafter, and it nearly brained me as I rounded the tables and headed towards the door. On the back swing, though, it hit the terrorist right in the middle of his forehead, and he went down, too.

When the front door burst open, I was sure more of them had arrived to finish us off, but it was only Howie Jameson and another man, one I'd met before on a previous case I'd solved. He's from Waynesboro's police department.

"Mrs. Dunlop!" Lieutenant Davis exclaimed in surprise as I all but collided with him.

"Mrs. Dunlop!" Howie said, somewhere between exasperation and disgust. "What's going on here?"

"These two men—" I gasped, pointing to Cleavor, who was struggling to roll from his back onto his knees, and the other one, still out like a dead fish, "—are dangerous! They thought Betty Jo here had their plastic explo—"

"How'd you know about the missing plastic?" Lieutenant Davis asked.

"—sive, and the President—" I tried to get in edgewise.

"She doesn't know anything," Howie said. "She never does."

"Oh, yes I do!" I reached into my carry-all, still sitting where I'd left it beside Betty Jo's table, and pulled out the magazine, then emptied the sheet of plastic explosive onto the blue-checked cloth.

That shut them up all right.

"By God, she's got it!" Lieutenant Davis declared in real astonishment. He picked it up gingerly.

"It's perfectly safe," I said kindly, to put his mind at ease if he didn't know how these things work. "Until somebody . . ."

"But how did *she* come by it?" Howie wanted to know.

"I got it from that woman who was here for lunch, the woman in the hat."

"*Hat!*" they exclaimed at the same time, and then looked at each other. "I thought you said HUT!" Howie said in an aggrieved voice. "The woman in *The Hut!*"

The lieutenant swore. My late husband would have turned in his grave. He didn't hold with saying such things in front of a lady. Not that he didn't have a fine range of swear words himself, when he hit his head on the hot water pipe or got his thumb caught in the back door. But I always pretended not to hear.

Howie nodded. "We were watching The Hut, but she came *here*, and she was wearing a *hat!*"

"Who?" Betty Jo asked, looking confused.

"Miss Gardener. She works in Waynesboro at a big company there. A pretty important job," Lieutenant Davis answered. "We've had word from the company's home office that she might be selling industrial secrets. A new coating for fibers. Then we were told that she was coming to Merton today to pass a sample block of the coating to whoever was paying her to steal it. These two, I guess. But by the time the message got to me, it read to watch for the woman in The Hut in Merton, then follow anyone she met there and handed a magazine to."

"Me," I said. "She gave it to me. There was a code she was expecting, and I accidentally used it. So she handed the magazine to me. With the plastic or whatever it is, in there between Wild Joy and Longevity Lashes."

"I don't believe it," Howie declared. "Nobody would think you're a *spy*."

"*She* did," I said hotly. "And what's more I can identify her again, hat or no hat. These two got rough with Betty Jo, here, thinking she was the woman they wanted. Because of her black hair bow, that looked like a hat to them. Morgan—that one—started in with the right words, then when she wouldn't answer, he said they'd paid her already and wouldn't be double-crossed."

Betty Jo nodded, still looking pale. Mrs. Clegg stood behind her now, one hand resting comfortingly on the girl's shoulder, the other hand clutching her husband's shotgun. Lieutenant Davis was busy handcuffing Cleavor and Morgan. They were still sort of dazed, as if they weren't used to being outwitted by widow ladies.

"There's a reward being offered by that company in Waynesboro," Lieutenant Davis was saying. "I expect you'll get it, Mrs. Dunlop."

And that pleased me no end.

Well, this time I didn't have my picture in the paper. There was no big trial because all three, that Miss Gardener and Morgan and Cleaver, took a plea bargain. Still, it shows you that my reputation is getting around. The ones I catch stay caught, and not even a smart lawyer can get them off.

My reward came last week. They said I'd saved the company a lot of money by getting back the secret formula of that fiber coating. So they gave me a tall pair of silver candlesticks and an engraved silver tray, all with the company's emblem on them.

Very nice, I'm sure, but I'd have rather had a big screen TV, to tell you the truth. And a dish antenna for the backyard, so I can keep up with what's happening in the world. Maybe next time I *will* save the President's life, and get invited up to the White House.

Which means I ought to keep an eye out for another nice hat.

Death at the Met

Naomi Strichartz

The ballet world was numb with shock. Edwin Carver, the English ballet master, choreographer and director of the Metropolitan Opera Ballet Company, was found dead backstage after a performance of his new ballet for the opera *Alcestis*. A dancer tripped over his body in the cross-walk and ran for help. Edwin Carver, otherwise known as Poet of the Gutter, had an international reputation for his sensitive, psychological ballets. He was disliked, however, as a person, and the question was not so much why he was killed as by whom.

Marya Cherkova sat on her comfortable chair mourning the loss of Carver. She was a great admirer of his ballet, *Elegy*, and now its talented creator was no more. Inspector Gabe Cohen was on his way to discuss the crime with her. Marya, formerly a ballerina with the famous Borsky Ballet, now worked professionally as a psychic and was often consulted by Inspector Cohen of the New York Police Department. Marya was no stranger to the Metropolitan Opera. The grand old house was her company's home when it played New York. Marya loved the large stage and iron staircases and she loved looking out into the box seats and seeing the priceless diamonds glittering in the darkened theater. It was overwhelming. She especially loved the roof-top studio where they rehearsed and took class. No one understood why Edwin Carver, who had choreographed for many major ballet companies, accepted a position at the opera, where ballet was so secondary. Marya suspected his well had run dry—no more juice was how she put it—and that he was worried about money. Secure, that was the Metropolitan, with its year-round salary and wealthy patrons.

The door bell rang and Marya got up to answer it.

"Madame," Inspector Cohen said, kissing her hand.

"Gabe, please, a murder has been committed, but do come in."

Marya was interested in keeping Inspector Cohen's advances at bay. It wasn't that she didn't like him, but that her life was very beautiful and complete as it was. Marya felt fortunate that working first for twenty years as a ballerina and now, at age sixty-one, a psychic, she never had to take a job she didn't love. Although she first began solving crimes for the police in order to supplement her income she now enjoyed combining her psychic talent with her incisive intellect. She called this a pleasure of a dubious nature. And to be drawn back again in time to the world of ballet was a bittersweet experience; nostalgia and joy intermingled with pain.

"Marya, you look lovely as usual," Inspector Cohen said, undaunted.

"Gabe, I thank you, but loveliness concerns me less than discovering who killed Edwin Carver."

Gabe nodded. "Edwin Carver was definitely murdered, stabbed to death by a sharp instrument, a knife, I presume. It happened some time after the opera last night. We will keep the cause of death a secret in case someone reveals his guilt by knowing too much."

"Yes, good. I assumed if the slaying occurred during the performance someone would have seen or heard something. Or felt something," Marya added with a shudder. "The cross-over is used by the whole company."

"Adele Gables is temporarily taking Carver's job. I have compiled a list of suspects for you to look over. Ms. Gables is of course on the list."

"Edwin had many enemies," Marya said, "professionally and in his private life. First we must go to the theater and see if there are any strong motives among the suspects. We establish the motive and then we will see."

"One dancer," Gabe said, "Beth Cleary, discovered the body."

Marya put on her poncho and they went out together to find a taxi. Considering the occasion it would not be too great an extravagance, especially since Gabe would pick up the tab.

The Metropolitan stood proudly on West 40th Street. Trucks were parked near the backstage as sets were changed for that night's production of *La Giaconda.*

Just like an ordinary day," Marya muttered, "as if nothing happened at all. The show must go on."

They walked through the stage door. Charles, the elevator man, remembered Marya from the old days. He was gnarled like an old tree and would probably be there forever. Marya tried to guess his age and gave up. Charles knew she would not take the elevator and smiled as they began the long climb up the winding staircases. They finally emerged on the roof-top studio which was beautifully lit with skylights. The cold, bright December sun danced patterns on the floor. The ballet company was rehearsing for the evening's performance and Madame Olga Grigorova was directing. Madame G., as she was called, ruled the rehearsal like a queen. She was dressed in a red leotard and matching long, sheer skirt. Her fishnet tights were the same color as her modified ballet slippers, which had a tiny heel. She didn't look like her seventy years until you got up close and saw her skin, stretched tight and thin, like that of an onion or old parchment. Her eyes were heavily made up, giving her an artificial, painted look. Madame had been ballerina of the Borsky Ballet years before Marya joined the company but had been forced to retire, quite young, because of a tragic injury to her knee. She stopped the rehearsal to greet Marya and the Inspector. The dancers, along with Madame G., looked shocked and disbelieving because of the news they had heard that morning. Adele Gables, ballet mistress, hovered along the sidelines checking schedules with the pianist and looking worried.

"We are taking a break," Madame G. announced, "so police can ask questions."

"Where is the dancer who found the body?" Inspector Cohen asked.

A tall thin woman stepped forward.

"Why Beth, hello," Marya said, recognizing still another face in this tiny world of ballet. "Tell Inspector Cohen and me exactly what you remember."

"I remained until the end of the opera because I had a walk on.

The ballet sequences were over and most of the company was already gone."

"Walk on ?" Marya asked, puzzled. "But Beth, surely you are soloist?"

"Yes, I am. Edwin liked to play games with me. He was punishing me for some offense or other. Oh, but I'll miss him."

"Darling, how terrible for you to find the body of your mentor!"

She nodded. "Edwin made me the dancer I am. I will never get over this."

"Beth, we must keep our heads if we are going to find the killer."

Beth nodded again, her face quite pale. She began to cry.

"Ms. Cleary, tell us exactly what happened last night," Inspector Cohen demanded, losing his patience.

"I did my walk on and then the opera was over. There was a lot of applause. I went to get out of my costume and realized I had dropped my head piece. The wardrobe mistress would kill me for that so I went back to look for it. That's when I tripped over his body in the cross-over. It was terrible."

"Did you see anyone else at this time?" Inspector Cohen asked.

"Who else from the company was there so late, you mean? Let's see. Adele was there, checking the stage. Some dancers complained they didn't have enough room. They had put the scenery in the wrong place. She was talking to Ned, the stagehand, about it. Tony Fuller, our dresser, was there collecting costumes and props."

"Oh, Tony Fuller used to dance with company, no?" Marya asked.

"Yes, but he retired, or rather was forced to retire this year because of his age. Because he turned forty."

"Since when does good dancer have to retire because he is forty?" Marya asked, indignantly.

"Since Edwin decided that would be the rule. I am past forty myself but Edwin made an exception for me. But it didn't stop him from torturing me about my age. I know I will be the next to go." She hesitated. "Oh yes, Madame G. was in the audience and then came backstage to congratulate the dancers, and of course Edwin also."

"Thank you Ms. Cleary, that will be all for now," the Inspector said, pausing until she was out of earshot. "How should we begin?" he asked Marya's advice.

"We will first watch rehearsal and then talk to all the suspects," Marya said, and not waiting for Gabe's exasperated response asked Madame G. to continue with the rehearsal.

Gabe prepared himself to be bored as the *Dance of the Hours* began, and eight men and women began to execute Madame's elegant steps. The dancers were not as technically strong as those in the Borsky Ballet but they had a sense of time and place, making them valuable to the opera. Marya enjoyed herself although Madame G.'s choreography was stilted and somewhat dated. The women bourréd delicately on point. They swayed and shifted, looking like bunches of colorful ribbons, and the men stood tall as handsome cavaliers. Somehow ballet must break free from all this in order to appeal to future generations, Marya thought. Marya watched with half her mind, while the rest of her scanned the studio for clues. Was Adele Gables glaring at Madame G.? Probably. Surely she wanted to choreograph this ballet herself. For how many years can one take orders, she wondered, not being good at this herself. And then there was Beth Cleary. She looked like a lithograph of a ballerina. She did not have enough juice, not enough talent, although she was still lovely. Even now she managed to look composed although tears rolled down her cheeks. She was devoted to Edwin Carver, but how he humiliated her! What a terrible way for him to repay her devotion.

Madame G. sat down next to Marya.

"Pale boy on the left, lover of Carver," she whispered. "And I am afraid of Adele, she wants to be choreographer."

"Was the boy his current lover?" Marya asked.

"No, several years ago, even before Tony. Now Carver is on a religious quest. Was," she corrected herself.

A half hour later, the perspiring dancers were dismissed.

"This is bad rehearsal," Madame said, "but I understand why. Tonight performance must be better."

Madame G. did not look too upset. Marya knew she despised Edwin Carver. She felt only Russians were capable of creating great work in the world of ballet. She was the most likely replacement for Carver's position but didn't seem to realize how damaging this looked. Adele must be a close second, Marya thought. Having worked at the Met for over twenty years she was so knowledgeable about it's repertory.

"So, what can I do for you?" Madame asked, arranging her red skirt so that her youthful legs were most visible.

"Why were you backstage last night after the premiere of *Alcestis*?" Inspector Cohen asked her.

"Why to congratulate, of course!" she answered, mildly outraged.

"Congratulate who?"

"Why the dancers. And Edwin also; it was his premiere and very successful," she said with distaste.

"Did you see Edwin Carver when you came backstage?"

"No. I couldn't find him. But I did congratulate the dancers; they will tell you. Ask them," she trumpeted imperiously.

Marya smiled fondly.

"Who do you think might have wanted to kill Carver?" Inspector Cohen asked her.

"Who? My dear, everyone! He was a bastard! He hurt everyone! A big mistake made by Metropolitan when they hire him. A big mistake!"

"Can you give us some examples?" Inspector Cohen asked.

"Of course! First, poor Beth. He tortured her. Ridiculed her in front of whole company. Took away her roles. Tell her she is too old to dance. Second, Tony. Such a good dancer. Fired for becoming forty. He must hate Carver! He must. Next, Adele. She wants job of boss, wants it badly. It is so stupid; she never even had a career! There are more. Believe me."

"Who will be the next director now that Carver is gone?" Marya asked.

"I would certainly hope it will be me," Madame G. snorted, "it should have been to start with."

"How are you managing?" Marya asked, meaning money.

"How? I teach at Carnegie Hall in the morning. Levensky's studio, for one dollar a student."

"Enough students?" Marya asked.

"No. I stage ballets for small companies. I try to convince Balanchine to hire me to teach. My savings get less and less, almost gone. I need this Met job," she said.

"You realize this makes you a prime suspect?" Inspector Cohen asked her.

"Yes. And also I hated his guts!" she finished triumphantly.

She got up with a huff and stalked out of the studio.

"She doesn't quite understand about the police," Marya said, chuckling.

Inspector Cohen followed her exit with an expression of distaste.

"Before we leave, I want to talk to Tony," Marya said.

"Tony?"

"Tony Fuller, the dresser. Remember?"

"Oh yes. Marya, you are so quick."

"I am," Marya agreed.

They went down three flights of turning stairs until they reached the wardrobe room. Racks of costumes were standing so close together it was hard to walk. Taffeta, satin and silk hung heavily on wooden hangers. Shelves sagged under wigs, spears, helmets and props of every description. The array of color made Marya dizzy; costumes in mauve, purple, green, yellow, blue and blood-red. She was sorry to have seen the latter. Several women were ironing in preparation for that night's performance. Finally she spotted Tony hanging up a costume that looked heavy. Probably *Traviata*, Marya thought, commiserating with the dancer who had to wear it.

"Marya," Tony exclaimed. "I am so glad to see you. Please, I need to talk to you alone." He was pale and shaking. The Inspector nodded and left the room.

"I'm terrified. Edwin Carver fired me last year. The whole company protested but it was no use. I'm afraid they will see I had a motive."

Marya sat down among the heavy skirts.

"So you're afraid the police think you are a suspect?"

"The dancers all know how upset I was, after dancing at the Met for seventeen years. Everyone knew about it. And I was seen backstage last night."

"Yes, you were," Marya agreed.

"And because the company knew Mr. Carver hated me . . ."

"Why?"

"Because I wouldn't sleep with him—anymore."

"Oh, I see. Tony, dancing is finished for you now. How are you managing?"

"Not very well," he said, his mouth bitter. "Please Marya, help me."

"Tony, I will try," she said, rising to meet Gabe in the hall. She found him pacing, like an expectant father.

"Now we go talk to Adele," Marya told him.

Inspector Cohen was baffled by the winding stairs and narrow corridors, and was more than happy to follow Marya back to the roof-top studio. Adele was leaning on the piano and poring over her spiral notebook. She was nervously puffing on a cigarette.

"Please put it out," Marya implored, refusing to step closer. Adele did so. She did not look sorrowful, Marya noted.

"Beth did it," she announced bluntly, in her mid-Western accent. "He finally got to her, God knows he worked at it."

Marya was shocked. "How do you know this?" she asked, sadly.

"He just took away her role in *Tannhauser*. Gave it to a seventeen year old! That is after removing her from the lead in *Aida* earlier this season. You know she followed him from American Ballet Theater where she was a soloist, just to work with him. What do you think?"

"I think Edwin must have hurt her deeply; but Beth kill him? Really I am shocked."

"He put her in a chorus in *Alcestis* along with three new girls. Treated her like a novice, instead of the fine soloist she is. I walked into a rehearsal one day and he was making her crawl on her knees. 'Pretend you are a dog chasing its tail' he told her. And when she finally did it, he laughed. How could she resist killing him?"

Edwin Carver was one of the greats; sometimes called Poet of the Gutter because he dared to delve into human passions, Marya mused. He would be missed by the ballet audience, if not by the dancers who knew him mainly for his cruelty.

"Ms. Gables, do you stand to gain anything from Edwin Carver's tragic demise?" Inspector Cohen asked.

"I don't know; perhaps. I wouldn't mind being in charge for a change. I've been here for twenty-two years."

"So long," Marya murmured, understandingly.

Adele did not look well. She was very thin, almost gaunt, with prominent cheek bones and so wrinkled skin. Her hair was gray and straw-like. She hasn't worn well, she is simply too thin, Marya thought, patting her round stomach with fondness. They don't eat, they smoke instead, and then feel deprived and needy.

"So you may be the next director of the Metropolitan Opera Ballet. That is quite a motive for murder," Inspector Cohen said.

Adele shrugged.

She is either ignorant or a good actress, Marya thought. Of course, a retired opera dancer would be able to act.

"We will wish to speak to you again," the Inspector informed her, leading Marya out of the studio.

Again shunning the hated elevator, Marya and the Inspector walked downstairs.

"Watch out!" Gabe shouted as a heavy crate crashed onto the staircase, barely missing them. Marya startled, stumbled, and fell to the landing below, the crate preceding her alarmingly. She stood up uncertainly, holding on to the bannister for balance.

"Marya, don't move! We have to check you for broken bones."

"Don't be ridiculous, I'm fine," Marya said, looking up to the landing above. She saw nothing.

Gabe grabbed his gun from his pocket and dashed upstairs. Soon he returned, shaking his head. It was completely quiet, unnaturally so. Marya pried open the crate which had been damaged in the fall.

"Bricks," she said. "Someone definitely does not want us here."

Inspector Cohen was upset and shaken. "Marya, Marya, I ask you to help the police and now I have risked your life! Perhaps this is too dangerous. Perhaps we should solve our own crimes. Are you sure you are all right?" he asked anxiously.

"Yes, fine. A bit shaky is all. So Gabe, don't worry. If in all these years, travelling all over the world dancing, nothing bad has happened to me, it certainly won't now!"

Inspector Cohen ignored the illogic of this remark and led her gently down the remaining staircases.

"Will you join me for a cup of hot tea? Come, it will calm us down," Gabe suggested.

"No Gabe, I can't. I am late to meet Zoya at the automat."

The Inspector, used to concealing his disappointment, bid her a reluctant good-day.

Marya glanced at the headlines as she walked uptown on 7th Ave. "Murder at the Met," read one. "Choreography King Slain." Ugh, she thought, walking faster. The air was cold and thin drops of sleet blew into her face and stung. Cars honked. Everywhere it was business as usual. The 57th Street automat always soothed her. Marya glimpsed Zoya sitting at their favorite table near the window, and waved. Zoya, her best friend through all those dancing years, when she was ballerina and Zoya was the company pianist. Zoya was still playing for the Borsky Ballet, while she, Marya, no longer able to dance, earned her living as a psychic. Perhaps I should have played the piano instead, she thought ruefully, but then quickly decided she would not exchange the fun she had dancing for anything.

"He is really dead?" Zoya asked after they kissed, Russian-style.

"You read it in the paper?"

"Yes."

"He is. And now I have to find out who killed him."

"Marya, not again! All these crimes are not good for you. But you won't listen to me. At least get some food so you will have the strength for this."

Zoya was already digging into a macaroni and cheese casserole. She had a cup of coffee and a slice of apple pie. Marya went to exchange some bills for nickels. How she loved the automat! She selected frankfurters and beans, a pastry with sweet sugar and cinnamon crumbs on top, and of course, hot coffee. Christmas decorations still hung limply on the walls although it was January fourth. Christmas for Americans, that was. For Marya, the Russian Christmas was yet to come, she thought, with happy anticipation.

"We will have a Christmas party as usual," Marya said to her friend, "murder solved or murder not solved."

"Certainly," Zoya agreed.

"And Zoya, this year party will be different. I will have a surprise."

Marya smiled and would say no more about it, but on her way out she mailed the invitations.

In the morning Marya decided to investigate backstage at the Met, in case the police overlooked something. As she walked across the massive stage she saw that someone had beaten her there. Madame Grigorova was frantically searching the area where Edwin Carver had been found dead. Marya quickly hid behind a scrim. She watched Madame G. grope on her knees for a few more minutes and then, with a furtive glance around, she exited. Marya went to the same spot and also found nothing. One of the stage-hands emerged from the wings.

"Why Ned! Hello," Marya said, feeling her color rise.

"Seems everyone is looking for something today; but I already found it."

"Please show it to me," Marya begged.

"Sure thing," he said, pulling a glittering brooch from his pocket. .

"Who was searching here, besides Madame G. and me?" Marya asked.

"Beth and Tony," he said. "And also Ned!" he added mischievously. "I got curious."

"May I have this for now?" Marya asked.

"Sure," he said, handing over the offensive object.

Marya was sure she recognized the brooch. Not the specific piece, which was in terrible taste, but the sort of thing. This was not a jewel Beth, or anyone else she knew, would wear. This was vintage Madame Olga Grigorova! Glancing at her watch, Marya decided she had enough time to get to Madame G.'s class at Carnegie Hall. It was cold and Marya wrapped her poncho more tightly around her. She walked briskly to 57th Street, but knew there was no time for a snack, thinking of her precious automat, with regret. Marya knew she no longer looked like a ballerina, since she was a bit heavy and quite unadorned. She dressed for comfort these days, favoring heavy cotton sweat pants in winter, with long-sleeved flowing tunics. But some balletomanes, seeing her handsome carriage and high, well-chiselled cheekbones, recognized her still.

Alas, at Carnegie Hall there was no choice but to take the elevator. At least John, the dear, dear elevator man, was still on the job. He must be eighty by now, Marya thought, breathing a little easier.

"Eight please," she said, grimacing.

"Never fear for John is here!" John said, smiling at her.

But Marya didn't fully relax until the door slid open on the eighth floor and she was once again on terra firma.

Levensky's School of Dance, the sign on the door read. Marya went in and there was Madame Grigorova, dressed to the hilt and surrounded by her entourage.

"Madame," Marya said, "I would love to watch class. Seeing

you at the Met has made me nostalgic."

Madame G. looked at her shrewdly. She was never a fool and she isn't now, Marya thought, reprimanding herself for being so transparent. She noticed that Madame was using her hands nervously and seemed not at all her usual flamboyant self.

"But of course, you will be our honored guest," she said, recovering.

"Any new protégés?" Marya asked.

"Yes, Tatiana," she said, pointing to a pretty girl with a neat brown bun and long, shapely legs.

"Tatiana? Is she Russian?"

"No, from Brooklyn!" Madame said, chuckling. "Her name is Judy, but Tatiana is so much nicer, don't you think?"

Marya agreed, smiling. She was ushered into the studio and given the "throne," a comfortable chair reserved for guests.

"Girls, this is Marya Cherkova, famous ballerina," Madame said, in a tone that suggested Marya was not, however, as famous as she herself.

Marya nodded graciously. Madame G. was wearing yellow today and the front of her leotard was covered with brooches similar to the one in Marya's purse. She had rings on almost every finger, large colorful stones, and wore a pair of sparkling rhinestone earrings. On her head she wore a yellow silk scarf to keep her hair back, and tucked into her skirt was an identical scarf, there for effect, Marya thought, watching it flow gracefully. Such a show for nothing, Marya thought, watching the five students do barre. Tatiana was promising and Madame fussed and fumed over her. The others had a lack of talent to varying degrees. One girl, with short achilles tendons, couldn't bend her knees properly, making the steps impossible to execute.

"She is so capable," Madame said, using her shorthand for hopeless and glancing significantly at Marya.

Madame was still too nervous; perhaps, thought Marya, she is embarrassed by her small class, or was she worrying about her missing brooch? Marya was sure it was hers. Who else would wear such a thing? And then, she had been searching for something this very morning. The students worked hard, and watched their teacher with admiration as she meticulously executed each combination. No one could come close to her technique, even now, Marya thought, looking at her lined face and sighing. The pianist, a slender, twitchy woman, was playing the adagio from the second act of *Giselle*. Madame became young again as she was transformed into a Willi, a spirit avenging her faithless lover. One movement blended into the next, and in Madame's eyes, the soul of a great dancer shone. Her extensions were no longer high and her feet did not point so sharply, but each movement was an eloquent poem, and Marya forgot the students were in the room. How could she tell Inspector Cohen about the brooch? How could she allow them to question Madame G. and perhaps arrest her? Maybe she should just give it back.

"How terribly amateurish," Madame reprimanded a student who fumbled.

Amateurish, that is me, if I allow myself to become unobjective, Marya thought, rebuking herself sharply.

"We hope you will come again," Madame said, when class was over.

"I would love to do that," Marya said, embracing the aging ballerina.

I must keep my mind open, Marya thought, as she caught the bus going downtown. Madame Grigorova, who had just taught five students for one dollar each, might easily be the next choice for director of the Metropolitan Opera Ballet. This, Marya had to admit, was a fine motive.

As Marya was finally preparing herself a belated lunch, the telephone rang.

"Marya, when can we get together to discuss this case?"

"Now is good time, Gabe. I have something I must tell you. Please come chez moi."

"Marya, as you know, I am always happy to breathe the same air as you."

"And Gabe, I have, unfortunately, something to give you. Perhaps you should come right away."

"I will be there in five minutes," the Inspector told her. "I am calling from around the corner."

Marya walked into her study with a sandwich and coffee. She sat down at her beloved pine table and prepared to eat. But something was wrong! The room felt like danger and Marya tensed her body. She saw a movement behind her massive gold drapes; the very drapes she pulled to shut out the world when she read Tarot cards for her clients. Someone was in her sacred space! Marya backed out of the room and ran towards her front door. She was startled when the doorbell rang. Inspector Cohen had never seen Marya so white. He burst into Marya's study and found nothing but an open window.

"Wait," Marya said, bending to pick up a notebook from behind the curtain. It was just like the spiral notebook Adele Gables had yesterday at rehearsal. "Yes, I am right," Marya said, examining it. "It lists rehearsal times for the next week. It must belong to Adele!"

"I suppose it must have dropped out of her purse. But what was she doing in your apartment, unless she is the one we are looking for?"

"Or someone wants to make us believe that," Marya pointed out.

"I can make some tea," Gabe offered, noticing that Marya's pallor was unimproved.

"No Gabe, we will drink cognac, it will be much better," Marya promised, producing two crystal glasses and a half-full bottle of Courvoisier.

Soon they were both feeling better, although Marya was still shaken.

Someone doesn't want me nosing around the Met," she said. "This someone came to frighten me only, or perhaps to implicate someone else."

"'Someone' may be the murderer," Inspector Cohen said, grimly. Marya nodded.

"Let's go over the whole thing," Marya said, "motives, passions and ambitions. But first, I must show you this." She went to her tote bag and produced the offensive brooch.

"Are you proposing to me?" the Inspector teased.

"Gabe, we must be serious. This, I regret to say, belongs to the great ballerina, Olga Grigorova."

"Where did you get it?"

"Ned, one of the stagehands, found it near the scene of the crime."

"You mean Olga Grigorova is our killer?"

"No Gabe, I don't think she is and I intend to prove it. But I must also admit I saw Madame G. near the spot where Edwin's body was found. She was searching for something, and I suppose it was this. I want to go over what we know about each suspect. If you like we can begin with Olga Grigorova."

"I would like that," Inspector Cohen admitted.

"All right. Madame Grigorova disliked Edwin Carver. She was insulted by his appointment as director and wanted this position for herself. In addition, she was backstage the night of the murder and then she came to retrieve something today at the scene of the crime. I have been fair, no?"

"Exceedingly so," Inspector Cohen said.

"Good. So now I can say I am sure Olga Grigorova did not do it; but I will keep an open mind."

The Inspector sighed.

"Our second suspect is Adele Gables. She has worked as an underling for twenty or more years. Never a great or even a good dancer, but she prided herself on being a good rehearsal director. How she longed to be the true director for a change! To not hover on the sidelines, to not take orders. She too hated Edwin Carver and wanted his position badly. I think she would be likely to be appointed now. She knows the repertoire well and has worked for so long with the dancers. Not talented, but very capable," she added, remembering Madame G.'s secret code and smiling. "Then there is Tony Fuller. A dancer at the Met for seventeen years, it was his whole life. He was a good dancer and used to be lover of Edwin's. He often got small roles. In the opera, where there is so little ballet, this made him quite respected. Then suddenly Edwin decides, dancers over forty—OUT! Isn't that cruelty? This is a terrible belief, that only the young can dance. Was it revenge, because, perhaps Tony had taken another lover? Tony is bitter. He has a strong motive, too."

"Marya, you think everyone has a strong motive!" Gabe complained.

"Only the suspects, and of course they do!" Marya said, regarding him pityingly. "So, now we come to Beth Cleary. A soloist who is also forty years old. She is Edwin's protégé but he was beastly to her. He adored her in his own way, but also adored making her suffer. He was a . . . cruel man," she said, sadly. "Edwin Carver wanted for other people, not himself, to lose their egos; this was part of his religion. Once I said to him, 'Edwin, when we lose ego, we are dead; don't you know that?' And he just smiled his thin smile. Such a terrible man to have such a talent," Marya said, shaking her head. "So Gabe, these are our suspects, and one of them does not want me around."

"You will have protection," Inspector Cohen said, stoutly.

"No, I will have a hot bath and go early to bed. And Friday night you will come to my Christmas Eve party,"

"Christmas Eve party? But Christmas was last week!"

"I thought I told you already, our Russian Christmas comes later, thirteen days later, and as I said, you are invited."

"Marya, I feel honored, but we must concentrate on this case."

"What makes you think I am not?" Marya asked, offended, while leading him firmly to the door.

On Thursday, Marya cancelled her clients so she had time to prepare for her party. Zoya came to help boil, bake and knead.

"Marya, again you involve me in danger," she said, shakily.

"Zoya, nonsense," Marya said, "Inspector Cohen will be here and we will enjoy ourselves, while I get such useful information."

"Do you think they will all come?" Zoya asked.

"I think they will be afraid not to come," Marya said, wisely. "I think they will all be here. Let's make the borscht today and also the pirogies."

Together they chopped cabbage, onion and mushrooms and rolled the rich buckwheat dough, boiled cabbages and beets, and stirred.

"I am ashamed to say the black bread and coffee will have to be from the bakery, but everything else we make from scratch," Marya said.

Marya slept fitfully that night, tossing and turning. Her dreams were fragmented and were trying to tell her something. 'It does not look good for Madame Grigorova, it does not look good for Madame Grigorova,' she woke up intoning this, like a lament. Madame Grigorova, why? Could she have killed Edwin, after all, out of hatred and envy? Marya remembered the Olga Grigorova of the past. The sound of the endless ovations after her brilliant Black Swan and the sound of the ambulance as she was carried out of the theater on a stretcher, her knee hopelessly shattered. How bitter she must be, Marya thought, living in forced retirement on her paltry salary. She remembered visiting Olga years ago while she was recuperating.

"Well, time marches on and soon I would have had to retire anyway," she had said. "This is over and I am wondering what will come next."

Marya had thought of these words when it was her turn to pack away her pointe shoes and begin a new life. Things did not look good for Madame Grigorova, but things were not always what they seemed.

"My God!" she exclaimed, rushing to the telephone. "Gabe?"

" Marya, it is only six o'clock. Is something wrong?" he asked anxiously.

"Gabe, I want someone following Madame Grigorova. She must not be left alone for a minute until she arrives tonight at my house."

"Oh, so Madame Grigorova did it after all?"

"No, Gabe, she did not do it! Her life is in danger."

"She will have protection then, until tonight," he said hanging up the phone.

Marya sat deep in thought. Now the finger seemed to point at Adele, Madame's only rival for the directorship. Or, Marya realized, fingering the notebook, someone hoping to incriminate her.

Evening finally came and Zoya was the first to arrive. She admired the small tree trimmed with delicate crystals and golden apples made of glass. The table sagged under its magnificent feast. Inspector Cohen was next, quickly followed by Beth and Tony, who arrived together, both looking ill at ease. Adele arrived late as the others were beginning to relax, assisted by glasses of Marya's best Russian vodka. Madame Grigorova made a fashionable and very delayed entrance escorted by a handsome young man. This was quite typical of her but Marya gave Gabe an appreciative smile. Madame G. looked quite at home with all this "Russianness."

"My, looks delicious," she said, as Marya took her coat and large feathered hat. Zoya sat in the corner looking worried.

"There is nothing to worry about," Marya assured her, while passing out salted herring on thinly sliced black bread.

"Let's eat, drink and celebrate, and also get to know each other better," Marya suggested, as they were seated around the bulging table. They began with hot borscht; soup made with beets, cabbage, dill and sour cream. Then came the blini, thin buckwheat pancakes filled with sweetened cottage cheese and topped off with strawberry jam. Kasha, boiled potatoes and pirogies followed. The pirogies were delicate masterpieces of dough filled with lamb, mushrooms and onions. There was a crisp cucumber salad all tangy with onion and vinegar dressing, and of course piles of black bread. Madame Grigorova was ecstatic, sampling everything and talking a mile a minute. Adele, on the other hand, was silent and sullen, while Tony and Beth looked anxious. If Madame's young man was unusually quiet, no one seemed to notice, since they were too preoccupied with their own thoughts. Everything got washed down with plenty of vodka and soon it seemed like a real party.

"What is that?" Inspector Cohen asked as Marya wheeled out her Samovar.

"The Russian way of making tea," she explained, putting black tea leaves into the urn and pouring boiling water over them. The tea was served with lemon and was very strong. The coffee cake was wonderful and even Zoya was more relaxed. Only Inspector Cohen and Madame G.'s young escort seemed watchful and alert. When no one could eat another bite, Marya poured cognac as an after-dinner drink.

"To Edwin," she toasted, waving her glass and looking around carefully.

"Amen," shouted Madame G., swaying and looking as though she might topple over. Tony looked uncomfortable and Beth began to cry. Adele got up to leave.

"I must be up early in the morning," she apologized.

"Please stay, you must," Marya said, firmly.

Adele sat down, looking at the door regretfully.

"So, Christmas Eve Russian-style," Marya began, "probably most of you are wondering, what do they do; first a feast, and then what?"

"I was wondering," Gabe said, raising an eyebrow at Marya.

"Good. Of course you all know that I am a psychic. Perhaps you don't know that my grandmother was also."

"Marya," Gabe said, warningly.

She glared at him. "At our house in Russia, when I was a child, after dinner on Christmas Eve, we would scry."

"Scry?" Beth asked.

"Yes, tell fortunes, but in a special way."

She rose to light a large red candle and closed the overhead lights. Then she brought out a bowl of cold water, a metal cup, and small pieces of beeswax. She pulled a pair of tongs out of her pocket. "First we melt wax over fire and then drop quickly into the cold water. We take out the shape with tongs and hold it between the candle and the wall. We see the shape it casts and we all guess what it is. Is fun," she assured them.

"Now," she continued, "one by one we will take spoonful of wax and throw in cold water." She illustrated this and then removed the resulting shape, which cast a large, eerie shadow on the wall. "I think—is a swan," she announced triumphantly.

"No, it looks more like a weird sort of dog," Beth said, giggling.

"So you see, we take turns and all guess, but I will guess last because, I am, after all, the psychic," she said, bowing her head immodestly.

"Marya, I wouldn't really think this is a good time for games," Inspector Cohen said, impatiently.

"I disdain to even answer," Marya said, glaring at him, "and for that, you get no turn! Zoyishka, why don't you start since you have done before?"

Zoya scooped up some hot wax in a spoon and dropped it in the water.

"A cupcake," she declared, holding up the resulting shape.

"No, a bee," Tony shouted.

"A spider, missing some legs," Adele said, getting into the spirit.

"I see a piano stool," Marya said, smiling. "Who is next? Perhaps Olga will go?"

Olga Grigorova had regained her sobriety after drinking a few cups of the strong Russian tea. She plopped her wax in cold water and held the result in front of the candle.

"Pirogie," she exclaimed, patting her full stomach.

"I see a pointe shoe," Tony said.

Gabe sat in the corner, sulking and saying nothing.

"I see a beautiful, shining brooch," Marya said, a bit too loudly.

Madame G. gasped and sat down unsteadily. Inspector Cohen lifted his eyebrows and began to pay closer attention.

"Adele, you are next."

Adele got up. Adele's wax shape looked like nothing at all and the company was quiet.

"A blob," Adele said, finally, "a blob from outer space."

"Why, I believe I see something," Marya said, "I see a rehearsal notebook. I think it belongs to you! One that you have lost."

Adele glared at her. "How did you know I lost my notebook?"

"I am a psychic," Marya said, "and also you lost it in my apartment!"

Inspector Cohen prepared to rise but Marya waved him back.

"Gabe, first everyone must have a turn. Beth, you are next."

"No, I won't play any stupid games, I won't. Edwin Carver is dead and you are all celebrating. I hate you all!"

"Oh? And didn't you hate Edwin too?" Marya asked.

Beth didn't answer but glared angrily at all of them.

"So Beth does not wish to scry. Tony, then it is your turn."

Tony took a lot of wax on his spoon and the result was quite pretty.

"A hat with feathers," he said, favoring that sort of thing himself.

"A tutu," Adele said with another nervous giggle.

"A birthday cake with candles," Madame G. offered, still fixated on food.

"No, it's a giraffe," Beth said, deciding to participate after all, "see the long neck?"

"Yes, I do see something long," Marya said, "But I see a long knife, like this one," and with that she suddenly pulled one from the pocket of her billowing tunic.

Tony paled, "I didn't do it, I hated him, but I didn't." He seemed to shrink before their eyes.

"I think you did," Marya said sadly. "In fact, I know you did. You see, we have carefully not revealed the cause of death to any of you. Only the murderer knew he committed this terrible crime with a knife. Although I suspected you, I did not know for sure until now. It was you, Tony, you killed Edwin and you planted Adele's notebook behind my curtain. You also threw a crate at me at the Met, although I believe you did not really intend to kill but just to frighten me."

"And it was me who lost her brooch and then panicked," Madame G. said.

"Yes, it was."

Tony began to sob uncontrollably.

Inspector Cohen's face had undergone a transformation, from scorn and impatience at Marya's methods, to astonished admiration.

"Marya, my God, Bravo!" he said as he and Madame G.'s escort led Tony from the room.

"Marya, my young friend said you have perhaps saved my life. I have been so frightened since the night of the murder. You see, I heard voices that night. Angry, fighting voices, Tony's and Edwin's. Then there was a muffled scream. I was on my way to congratulate the dancers. I hid behind the curtain, frightened. My brooch caught on the curtain and fell to the floor. I couldn't see clearly but was sure Tony saw me and heard me as I ran from the wings. Tony probably thought, good, I'll leave brooch there and they will think Olga is the murderer!"

"I think that is true, Madame, but he must have liked you better than he liked Adele, because when he stole her notebook, and planted it here in my apartment, he was casting suspicion on the only other person in a position to become director of the company. It took attention away from him. And now I can return this to you," Marya said, handing over Madame's brooch.

"As a token of my appreciation I want you to have it," Olga Grigorova said, grandly, "and Merry Christmas!"

Solemnly, Marya placed the atrocious object on her tunic and, holding back her laughter, she bid her tired guests good night.

That's All, Folks

Linda Wagner

I was sitting in my office staring out the window at the street below. It was midsummer in Cleveland, Ohio and we were having a spell of ninety degree-plus weather. My investigative practice was in the doldrums, the air conditioning was working only sporadically and it seemed that even the pigeons perched on the window ledge were sweating.

The phone rang. "Spotlight Investigations, Livia Lewis speaking," I answered in my best female detective at-the-ready voice.

"This isn't Little Caesar's Pizza?" a young man's voice asked.

"No, it's not. You have the wrong number."

"Are you sure?"

"This is a detective agency. I own it. If I were also selling pizza, believe me, I would notice." Why is it that people don't like to accept the fact that they've dialed the wrong number? I hung up the phone and went back to concentrating on being uncomfortably warm.

The phone rang again. "Spotlight Investigations," I answered with a little less enthusiasm.

"I'd like a large pizza with mushrooms and sausage." A woman's voice this time.

"You have the wrong number."

"I do?" she said, sounding genuinely amazed. "Is this 555-1800?"

This was becoming annoying. "Yes, it is. But it is not a pizza place, it's an office." I hung up. Must be a lot of sunspot activity today, I thought. I looked at the phone. It rang again.

"Spotlight Investigations," I answered irritably.

"I'm sorry," a deep male voice replied, "I have the wrong number."

"Wait," I said, "are you trying to order a pizza? Are you dialing 555-1800?"

"Well, yes, that's the phone number on the flyer."

"This is the number, but it has nothing to do with pizza."

He laughed. "I hope you enjoy meeting new people by phone," he said, "because they've passed out a lot of these."

I hung up thinking that I have often complained that my phone doesn't ring often enough, but this was not what I had in mind. I was mulling over how complicated it would be to change my business phone number when the thing rang again.

I grabbed it. "This is not, I repeat, this is NOT Little Caesar's Pizza!" I yelled crankily.

"Livia, have you gone over the edge?" It was my mother's voice. This was the only call I wanted less than another pizza order.

I wiped the sweat from my upper lip with a tissue. "Oh, hi, Ma. Some pizza place handed out flyers with the wrong phone number on them. People have been calling here to order pizza."

"So, maybe God is trying to tell you something, Nancy Drew. Better learn to cook instead of doing this girl detective thing."

Had I been a really evil person in my last life or what? "How did this immediately get to be a discussion of my profession? And why do we keep having to have this same discussion?"

"Don't be sassy, young lady!"

"Yes, ma'am." I scuffed a mental toe. How many good deeds was I going to have to do before I could become a real girl? Beyond that, how many to become a real woman?

"We're having a family barbecue Sunday."

She has these little family gatherings every so often in the summer to torture me. "I hate eating outside, Ma. Dirt gets in your food. You chase your napkin around while batting at various venomous insects. It's no fun." I didn't mention the worst part. The family.

"You are coming, Livia. Although, I have to admit that it *is* getting embarrassing, your not being married. You're the only one your age without children," she said pointedly.

"I'm thinking of getting a dog," I answered defensively. I saw that we were going to have the whole nine yards, profession, marital status and failure as a female.

"Be here Sunday at three, Livia, " she said imperiously.

"Gee, Ma, I've got an awful lot of paperwork and stuff . . .. " I am daughter, hear me whine.

"You will be here. I'll see you then." She hung up before my lips could form another protest. I flipped on the answering machine before anything else could happen.

There was a soft knock at the door. Now what, I thought. "Come in," I said aloud.

She entered hesitantly. She was a tiny woman wearing a beautifully embroidered peasant dress that went down to her ankles. Her long salt-and-pepper hair was tied back and hung straight down her back. She stood with her hand on the doorknob, looking around the office, taking everything in with sharp narrowed brown eyes.

"Come in," I repeated. She came forward, her movements somewhat birdlike. She perched on the edge of the chair in front of my desk.

"Miss Lewis?" she asked. I nodded. "My name is Harriet Rigby. I want you to follow my husband."

"Geez, I hate divorce work. I usually don't . . ."

"This is not about divorce," she said firmly, as if it were an unusually silly notion. "I think," her eyes darted around the room, as if confirming that we were alone. Leaning forward she whispered, "I think that my husband is a bank robber."

"Excuse me?" I said, doubting that I could have heard it right. "Please speak up. No one is going to hear you."

She spoke a little louder. "I believe that my husband, Larry, is in the business of robbing banks."

"What makes you think so?"

"I was watching one of those true crime things on television. You ever watch them?"

I shook my head. "No, I don't have too much time for TV." Actually, considering my line of work, I find that type of television a touch exploitive, but I didn't think it was my place to judge in this situation.

"Oh, but they're really great," she enthused. "You have no idea how many criminals are actually caught because someone . . ."

"Your husband, Mrs. Rigby. What does this have to do with your husband possibly being a bank robber?"

"Why everything! As I said, I was watching this crime show and I was surprised when one of the stories was about some bank robberies here in Cleveland. You know, it's always amazing to see your hometown on television. The city didn't look half bad. The Terminal Tower and the BP building—"

Good God, this woman made my mother look like a second rater at sliding off the subject. "Mrs. Rigby," I said, interrupting her rambling narrative tour of the city. "Mrs. Rigby, please. About your husband."

"I'm getting to that. So, anyway, there was this story about a series of bank robberies, all apparently committed by the same robber. I paid more attention to the details because it was local and you never know.

"I was struck by the fact that the man's general build seemed a lot like Larry's. Of course, the robber wears masks, a different Looney Tunes character each time, so you couldn't see his face in the bank camera videotapes. Now, here's the thing . . ."

At last, we were getting somewhere. "Yes," I prompted, hoping to get there quicker.

"Larry is out of town a lot. He works for this novelty company and has to go on buying trips. He has to find suppliers for stuff like whoopie cushions, fake vomit, flies in ice cubes. Once he even—"

Where had I lost control? "I get the picture, Mrs. Rigby. Why do you think this Looney Tunes robber is your husband?"

"The dates, of course," she said as if speaking to a rather dull child. "The last two robberies were on dates when I am sure that Larry was supposed to be out of town. And, get this . . ." She brought her hand down on my desk with a bang. I jumped. "I found a Porky Pig mask in his sock drawer!" Wow.

"Now that really doesn't prove—" I began.

"Miss Lewis," she said using that tone again, "we have no children and there's no masquerade party in our immediate future. What possible reason could Larry have for possessing a Porky Pig mask?"

She had a point there. "Have you asked him about it?"

"How could I ever explain looking in his sock drawer?"

Silly me. I forgot how private a man's sock drawer can be.

I agreed to tail Larry, who was going out of town the following Monday. Too late to save me from the family barbecue, but whoever said life was fair? The air conditioner gave a final sounding clunk and shut down completely. Yeah, fairness wasn't an issue in real life.

Sunday, the day designated for the fun family get together dawned bright and sunny . . . and unmercifully hot. Great. The family that sweats together sweats together. I decided that I would arrive fashionably late, bolt a burger and leave unfashionably early.

A yardful of people turned to look as my battered MG pulled into the drive. The badminton game stopped dead in its tracks. Boy, if I was going to tail someone, maybe I'd better rent a car that attracted less attention. Or was it just that the members of my family were sort of single-minded?

I stepped gingerly out of the car, mindful of their attention, doing my best not to hit my head or trip. "Uh, hi, folks," I called. Several of them waved and called back. I was grateful when the badminton game resumed and everyone went back to doing what they had been doing when I arrived. My mother bustled over to me.

"Are you by yourself, dear?" she asked sweetly.

"No, Ma, I've brought my invisible rabbit, Harvey." Uh oh, I wasn't starting out too well, was I?

"You're late enough," she said a little huffily. "I thought maybe you were picking up a date."

"You didn't think I'd been killed in my awful little car? That's a switch." Suddenly I couldn't seem to control my mouth.

She took my elbow a little tighter than necessary and led me toward the happy family group. The smell of charred burgers was already in the air, and if the EPA was doing its job, there was a large fine and possible imprisonment in someone's future. The smoke hanging over the yard certainly appeared to be toxic.

"Look who's finally here," she called out to all and sundry. I mumbled amenities until my eyes just about crossed and prayed that the food would soon be burned enough to eat.

"So, you're still single, huh?" That was small talk from my

cousin, Mary Jean. She bent down to stop her three-year-old daughter from eating a caterpillar. The four-year-old was clinging to the back of her skirt, going through his shy phase. "Don't you want to have kids?"

"Sure, someday," I replied, dodging a small child who had run straight at me with a fudgesickle dripping down his arm.

"You'd better get a move on," Mary Jean continued. "Janie, don't put that in your mouth!" She took a dirt-covered stick out of the child's hand. "Remember, that old biological clock is ticking."

"Not fast enough," I said under my breath as the little group moved on to harass some other relative. A bumble bee strafed me, so I figured I'd better move on, too.

"Hot enough for you?" my Uncle Ed inquired as I passed the grill. Ed's department was cooking, not original thought.

"Naw," I answered. "It needs to be at least fifty degrees warmer. That food going to be ready soon, Uncle Ed?" He nodded, grinning. Oy.

In due course, the food was actually completed to my uncle's satisfaction. I put something on my paper plate that looked like it might have turned up in the aftermath of the Dresden Firebombing. I felt a little sorry for it, thinking that it had probably begun life as a hamburger.

I managed to choke the thing down without losing any fillings. At one point, I made a grab for my napkin which was blowing in the wind and, in the process, caused my paper plate to do a double gainer landing greasy side down in my lap. If you must do this grill thing, why can't you at least do the eating part inside where you have some control over the environment?

All things considered, it was one of the less painful family get- togethers I'd been to. I was there a total of an hour and a half, then I waited until my mother was distracted and removed myself from the premises as quietly as possible. She would be outraged that she hadn't had more time to torture me, but I had better things to do, like count the tiles on my living room ceiling.

I was waiting at the foot of his driveway the next morning when Larry Rigby's car pulled out. He was driving a red BMW and it stuck out in traffic pretty well. According to Harriet, he had said he was going to Columbus and would be back the following evening. If he was going to Columbus, he was already going in the wrong direction. I followed him to a parking garage on Chester Avenue near midtown. He pulled in and I waited outside the pedestrian doorway, checking each person who emerged from the garage on foot. I watched for nearly an hour. No Larry.

Pulling into the garage myself, I looked up and down each row of parked cars. After a few minutes, I located the BMW. It was empty. How had he gotten past me? A quick check with the attendant confirmed that the door I had been watching was absolutely the only one where someone on foot could leave the building.

I sat in my car for another forty minutes or so, just in case, but I could only conclude that he had eluded me and was already on his way to whatever his real destination was. My car was getting like a blast furnace as the sun moved overhead, so I decided to give it up and tell Harriet Rigby we'd have to wait until next time. Whatever her husband was into, it wasn't worth my having a stroke over it.

Back at the office, my answering machine yielded a large number of hang up calls. I knew that they were people who thought they were going to order a pizza when they had dialed the number. This was confirmed by the last caller, a gruff sounding man who muttered something about a "goddamned misprint" before hanging up. I was going to have to bite the bullet and have my number changed.

I called Harriet Rigby and reported that I had somehow lost her husband at the parking garage. "Larry turned out to be a little more slippery than I had anticipated," I said.

After a short, but decidedly disapproving silence, she spoke. "All right. You'll have another chance Thursday. He's doing another overnight. This time it's supposed to be Pittsburgh."

I agreed to take up the tail again, telling her that since I now knew what to expect I wouldn't lose him a second time. This mollified her somewhat, but she still wasn't happy.

"I just want an end to this," she said and hung up without saying goodbye.

I switched on the answering machine quickly to avoid both my mother and an onslaught of wrong numbers. Things were not going well. And it was still beastly hot. I could arrange for the phone number change from home where at least I had a couple of reliable fans.

Thursday morning I was waiting for Larry when the BMW

pulled out again. The heat had abated somewhat and I was cheered by the fact that there hadn't been any bank robberies during the time that Larry had been away from home. I was beginning to suspect that something other than robbing banks was on his agenda.

Once again I followed the red car through morning traffic to the same parking garage on Chester Avenue. This time, though, I followed him in. Parking a few spaces down from where he pulled in, I watched as he got out of the BMW and into the car next to it, a gray Ford Escort. There was no evidence of cartoon characters, yet, but this guy was sure up to something.

He was harder to follow now in the more ordinary car, but I managed to keep him in sight. Soon we moved into a residential area and the traffic thinned considerably. I slowed my car and let him get a couple of blocks ahead. I watched as he turned into the driveway of an average looking, middle class bungalow. I parked across the street and waited.

Larry got out of his car, went straight up to the front door. Pulling a key out of his pocket, he opened it and went in. I hung around for a few minutes, but decided things would keep until next morning. I was pretty sure I knew what was going on now. It was illegal, but it had nothing to do with robbing banks. I'd give the guy one more night.

The next morning I drove back to the house early and parked in the same place as the previous day. When Larry came out of the front door, I called his name. He looked puzzled, but walked over to the car.

"Hi, Larry," I said. "How ya' doin'?"

"I'm okay. Uh, do I know you?"

"No, but Harriet does."

He looked unhappy. "Harriet?" he repeated.

"Harriet Rigby. Your wife. Or should I say one of your wives? Have any kids here, Larry?" He was looking pretty miserable. "Get in," I said. He walked around to the passenger side and got in. "Look, Larry, you've got to talk to me. Harriet thinks you're out robbing a bank."

"What? That's ridiculous! Who are you anyway?"

"I'm Livia Day Lewis. I'm a private detective. Harriet hired me. As I said, she thinks you're a bank robber." He sat there, chewing on his lip, looking trapped. "Talk," I said emphatically.

"Okay, okay." He wiped the sweat from his forehead with a

handkerchief. The weather was turning hot once more. That, combined with his steadily increasing nervousness was making him sweat profusely. "You're right," he said. "I am married to both of them. My name is Larry Franklin here. I married Emily first. We have two kids, a boy and a girl. I never had kids with Harriet. I didn't think it would be fair."

Help me please! "Fair? Larry, do you understand that what you're doing here is illegal?"

"I'm not hurting anyone," he pouted. "Why should anybody care about this? You're not going to tell Harriet, are you?"

"Not only do I have to tell Harriet, I have to tell the police," I said.

"But why? I love them both. I'm taking care of them all. I love my kids. If I go to jail, everybody gets hurt."

I wished he would stop talking. He was starting to make sense to me and that was a bad sign. Maybe the heat was melting my brain. "All right," I said, certain that I would hate myself in the morning. "We'll make a deal. I won't tell the cops, but you have to pick one wife and underline!"

He sighed. "I will. Thank you. Thank you so much!" He got out of the car. "What made Harriet think I was robbing banks?" he asked.

"Porky Pig in your sock drawer," I said and pulled away.

Two days later, I was clearing up some paperwork in the office. The heat wave was continuing. The air conditioning was functioning, but the telephone was making my life unbearable. Thanks to some nearsighted printer, I had had to change my phone number. Of course, this meant I also had to change business cards, stationery and God knew what else. But, then I love life's little challenges, don't you?

I called my mother to give her my new number. Big mistake. I had completely forgotten that I would also be giving her the opportunity to chew me out for my arbitrary departure from the family burnt offering ceremony. My ears were going to ring for a week. The phone, however was ringing in the here and now.

"Spotlight Investigations, Lewis."

"This is Larry Franklin, er, Rigby."

"Oh, yeah. The friendly neighborhood bigamist. What did you decide?" I asked.

"Well . . . I told Harriet. She cried. Then she said she wouldn't let me go. She loves me too much. So, I told Emily, you know, to be fair."

"I like fairness in a man, Larry."

"Thank you," he said sincerely. "Anyway, Emily wouldn't agree to let me go either. Neither of them liked the idea of us all living together, so . . ."

"So, you want to continue the time sharing arrangement," I finished for him.

"Yes, we want to. That is, if you . . . I mean . . ."

I laughed. Who was I to destroy a situation in which everyone seemed to be happy? How many people get to be happy for even a while? Let their respective analysts sort it out later. "Larry," I said, "if everyone involved is content, then I won't be the one to tinker with your lifestyle. If it ain't broke, don't fix it."

"Thank you," he said. I could hear the tears in his voice.

I had to ask. "By the way, Larry, what *was* Porky Pig doing in your sock drawer?"

"Well," he said hesitantly, "actually, it was a surprise for Harriet. She had complained that our lovemaking had become just a little, uh, commonplace and so I thought maybe, you know, some kind of fantasy thing like wearing a mask might make it more exciting. I had no idea that there was a bank robber out there with the same idea. Weird, huh?"

"Yeah, weird. Nice talking to you, Larry." I hung up realizing that I was smiling for the first time all day.

The Death of a Much-Travelled Woman

Barbara Wilson

It is a commonplace that in this world there are tourists and then there are travellers. Yet within the latter category, at least three distinctions are possible: There are the great travel writers like Jan Morris and M.F.K. Fisher, who delight in words as much as famous sights and cities and are inclined less to the rigors of the adventurous life than to the luxuries, poetic or squalid, of foreignness, exile and history; there are the great travellers—Freya Stark, Gertrude Bell and, farther back, Mary Kingsley and Isabella Bird (a frail Victorian lady whose husband said of her, "She has the appetite of a tiger and the digestion of an ostrich.")—women who could not and cannot stay still and who seek out the bizarre and the prohibited; and then there are the travellers, not very great, who write books, not very literary ones.

Edith "Tommy" Price was that last sort of traveller, that last sort of writer. And I'd adored her.

I'd grown up reading her books. My aunt Eavan, who was something of a traveller herself, having ventured to Alaska before the cruise ships and Hawaii before the hordes, was a great fan of Tommy Price's and had collected all her books and sent copies on to me from the time I was eleven or twelve. *Jungle Journey, To the Top of the Very Top*, and *Lost in the Interior* were my favorites. For years they'd been out of print, but the British publisher Harridan had recently relaunched two volumes in a handsome new paperback edition, and interviews with Tommy Price had begun to appear in everything from the *Guardian*'s Women's Page to *Spare Rib*.

She sounded such a dashing, risk-taking, literate woman that I determined to meet her. As an itinerant translator I have travelled widely myself, but not always adventurously, at least not intentionally. My idea of foreign intrigue is an attractive woman at the next cafe table. I do admire my more intrepid sister voyagers, however, and have a nodding acquaintance with many. Therefore I wrote to Tommy Price at her home in Dartmoor and proposed a visit. I said I was in the process of translating her book, *Bound for Greenland*, into Spanish for an Argentinian publisher. This was not an entire falsehood. My dear friend Victoria, who runs her own Argentinian publishing house, *should* be publishing Tommy Price, and I'd have to make a note to persuade her one of these days.

A reply came immediately and briefly: "Tuesday, December 1, I shall be at home from three o'clock. Please join me for tea. Yours sincerely, Tommy Price."

I took the train to Exeter the morning of Tuesday, December 1, and then hired a car for the hour's journey to the small village of Sticklecombe-in-the-Moor. December was a bleak and glorious time of year to visit Dartmoor, and it was an appropriately bleak and glorious day, with wind sweeping over the yellow gorse and purple heather and sun breaking out dramatically behind the great rock piles, the granite formations called tors. It had been many years since I'd been in this part of the country; the last time had been with Sheila Cragworth, who was at the time nursing a desperate passion for a married woman and hoped to lose herself in the close study of geology and Neolithic archeological remains. I'm afraid I also learned perhaps more than I wanted to know about the way hot lava had once bubbled up to the surface where it cooled to become granite, and about the hut circles, barrows, monoliths, dolmens, menhirs and kistvaens of the ancient people who once inhabited this severe landscape. It had been forested then; now it was bare and dramatic, with bogs and rivulets, granite rubble, and herds of Dartmoor ponies roaming freely through the military firing ranges.

Sticklecombe-in-the-Moor is an old market village hidden in a wooded valley by a river. It has a stone church, numerous tea shops and at least one four-star pub for the walkers who throng to Dartmoor in the summer months. The address Tommy Price had given me was down a narrow lane with thick stone walls on either side. As I drove cautiously along, a wild rain burst out, and an oncoming car, in a great hurry, almost sideswiped my rented Ford Escort.

That was irritating, but not quite so irritating as arriving at Tommy's cottage to find no one at home. I stood on the step knocking loudly, wondering if she were deaf, or if she were the sort of woman who would deliberately invite a stranger to Dartmoor and leave her standing wretchedly in the rain outside. I remembered she had written in *Lost in the Interior* :

"At times, I know not why, a perversely asocial sensibility comes upon me, and I find myself doing and thinking things completely at odds with received notions of good behavior. It is precisely this misanthropic and contrary streak in my character which has enabled me to turn my back on civilization for months at a time and to embrace hardship and solitude with equanimity. Alas for my friends and family, however: the suddenness of my mood changes, the violence of my anti-social emotions!"

Alas for Cassandra Reilly, standing on the step and becoming more and more soaked, the unwitting victim of a burst of antisocial contrariness!

Well, I could be contrary too. I returned to the car, found a bed and breakfast not far away and changed my wet clothing. My landlady made me a cup of tea and commiserated about the failed visit to Tommy Price.

"She's not what you would call a friendly sort," Mrs Droppington said. "Keeps to herself, she does."

"Has she lived here long?"

"Long and long. The cottage belonged to her brother, who retired here in the thirties. But he's been dead, oh, twenty years now. Miss Price keeps the place up, I'll say that for her, but that's mainly the work of her friend, Miss Root."

"Miss Root?"

"Oh yes, childhood friend, I understand. Constance Root. She has always taken care of Miss Price's things while Miss Price was out gallivanting around the world."

None of the books had ever mentioned a Constance Root.

"And is Miss Root a friendly sort?"

"The two of them keep to themselves mostly, but when Miss Price is away, I'd say Miss Root is friendlier."

I set out again for the Price-Root household about five, in the darkness of an early evening thick with rain. Familiar country smells of animals and manure mixed with the acid scent of peat and bog from the hills above us. Sheila Cragworth had not believed any of the folktales and horror stories that abound in Dartmoor, about the Wisht Hounds and the ghosts and pixies, but I, granddaughter of Irish immigrants to Chicago, couldn't help a shudder creeping back and forth across my shoulders, as I squished along the short road from Mrs. Droppington's. Dartmoor had been a place of great religious significance once, but all that was left were superstitions. I remembered reading that the only way to deal with pixies was to take off one's coat, turn it inside out and put it on again.

It was too cold for that and so I only hurried on. This time I found a light on in the cottage window, a light that hadn't been there earlier.

I knocked. I knocked hard. And harder.

At length a gray head appeared in the window at the top of the door, and a low voice asked cautiously, "Who is it?"

"Cassandra Reilly. I had an appointment with Tommy Price for tea a few hours ago. But no one was here when I arrived, so I've come back."

The door slowly opened and a woman in her early eighties stood there in a plain dress with a heavy shawl and slippers on her feet. The stay-at-home, I thought, Miss Root who keeps the home fires burning while Miss Price is out writing books about her adventures.

"Please come in out of the rain," she said at length, when she could see I wasn't moving. "Miss Price isn't at home, I'm very sorry."

I stepped into the vestibule and couldn't help craning my neck for a view of a cozy-looking sitting room stuffed with books.

"She left very suddenly," the woman said.

I remembered the car that had almost sideswiped me in the narrow lane: Tommy Price on a sudden mission to Borneo perhaps.

"I can offer you some tea," Miss Root said. "I'm afraid I live very simply when Tommy is not here."

She invited me into the sitting room.

"Oh look," I said, going immediately to the bookshelves. "The original editions of *Out Beyond Outback* and *Kangaroo Cowboys*. I loved those books when I was a girl; I longed to go live in Australia."

A faint glimmer of pleasure drifted across Constance Root's wrinkled features, replaced almost immediately by one of disapproval. "Well, they're terribly outdated now. The modern day reality is surely quite different. I watch television and read the papers and what Tommy described is not to be found in Australia today. I can't imagine why anyone would be interested in republishing such fairy tales."

"Oh but that's part of the charm," I said. "We like to imagine a world where everything seemed simpler, where a traveller could come upon an enchanted place and describe it like a fairy tale. Nowadays it's all Hiltons and package tours."

Miss Root shook her head and went to put the kettle on for tea. I took the opportunity to scan the bookshelves for other favorite books. Tommy Price had a wonderful library of women's travel stories. Here were some of the classics: *Bedouin Tribes of the Euphrates* by Lady Anne Blunt; *My Journey to Lhasa* by Alexandra David-Neel; *Dust in the Lion's Paw*, the autobiography of Freya Stark; *A Lady's Life in the Rocky Mountains* by Isabella Bird; and here too were hard-to-find, wonderful titles like *On Sledge and Horseback to Outcast Siberian Lepers* by Kate Marsden (1883), and *To Lake Tanganyika in a Bath-Chair* by Annie Hore (1896) and *Nine Thousand Miles in Eight Weeks: Being an Account of an Epic Journey by Motor-Car Through Eleven Countries and Two Continents* by Mildred Bruce (1927). Yes, and here were the complete works of Tommy Price detailing her travels to Greenland, the Amazon, Tibet, Ethiopia, Australia—all written in the tough, no-nonsense prose that had so delighted me in my youth.

I opened *Kangaroo Cowboys* and read at random:

"It wasn't long before Jake guessed I was not the fearless British ex-soldier I had made myself out to be. 'Why,' he said to me one day as we were riding alongside each other through the bush, 'You're a lady, ain't you?'"

Miss Root came back in with a tea tray and I told her enthusiastically, "One of the things I really loved about Tommy Price was her disguises. Half the time she was masquerading as a man but she also loved to get herself up in any kind of native costume.

Do you remember how she disguised herself as a harem girl to get into the Sheik's inner sanctum?"

"Oh yes," said Constance dryly. "Tommy was quite the quick-change artist."

"I hadn't realized she was still travelling," I said. "Where's she off to this time?"

"The city of Pagan in Burma," Constance said. "She said she had an old friend there she wanted to see. At her age she's trying to pack in as much as possible."

The disapproving look came over Miss Root's wrinkled face again. I wondered how it must feel to be always left behind.

"You've known Miss Price a long time, I gather?" I said.

She shook her head and said, "More tea?"

I returned to Mrs. Droppington's farm house and spent the evening curled up with *Kangaroo Cowboys*, which Constance Root had insisted I take.

"It can't make up for having come all the way from London, but please take it anyway. I know Tommy wouldn't mind."

The next morning I decided that I'd take a walk on the moors before returning to Exeter and London. I was disappointed not to have met Tommy Price, but felt inspired all the same. Would I still be on the go at eighty, visiting pagodas in the jungle? Or would I have retired to some quiet village like Sticklecombe-in-the-Moor? I had never been a true adventurer except in spirit; I liked a bitter-sweet espresso and a good newspaper far better than a jungle teeming with scorpions and snakes.

Mrs. Droppington fixed me a hearty country breakfast and warned me about straying too far from the paths.

"The mists and rain can come sudden up here. There's plenty of folks lost in Dartmoor every year."

I promised to be careful and took the Wellingtons and oilskin slicker she pressed on me, as well as a sandwich and thermos of tea for later. It was a clear morning, sunny and brisk, just right for walking, and I set off in good spirits, dutifully sticking right to the paths. The hills above Sticklecombe-in-the-Moor had a number of famous tors, those masses of bulging granite that look in some cases like great fists pushing their way up from the earth and in other cases like Easter Island gods, with enormous noses and full lips. To gaze out across the landscape was to feel in a very wild place, at the top of the world, but the ground itself was hard going, being covered with what is called clitter, the rubble from outcrops of granite, and squelchily wet. Dartmoor is poorly drained; the land is like a sponge, with bogs among the tussocks of purple moor grass and tufts of whortleberries and wild thyme.

I walked for several hours, seeing few signs of life except for the occasional pony and, high above, the lark or stone curlew with its eerie cry. I had hoped to see some of the hut circles that Sheila Cragworth had been so keen on all those years ago, but all I saw were a few moorstones, the old stones along the ancient path that had been erected by villages like Sticklecombe-in-the-Moor centuries ago to help travellers find their way across the stretches of high ground. I remembered how irritating Sheila had found my superstitious bent. Poor old Sheila; she was now some sort of Tory functionary in Brighton, which showed what a broken heart could do to you.

I had lunch next to a particularly impressive tor that looked like a Northwest totem pole with a raven's beak and a bear's torso and finished *Kangaroo Cowboys*:

"Someone once said to me, Why travel? After all, there's nothing new to discover, no place where no one has been before. To that I would say that more than half of travel, perhaps ninety percent of travel, is imagination. Some people can stay home and live lives of great adventure; others may roam the entire globe and yet remain as provincial as a country lad. What you get out of travel is what you put into it; and if you put your whole imagination, you will get a great deal."

I had difficulty reading the last words and raised my head to realize that, quite suddenly, the weather had changed.

An opaque white cloud was pouring over me like a sift of flour; but this cloud was wet and thick. It blanketed out the sun, the path and even the tor at my back. Within a few minutes I couldn't see my boots in front of me. The fog quickly crept under my collar and through my clothes, until I felt chilled all over. I stood up, but had no idea which direction to move, or whether to chance moving anywhere. Shapes and sounds were completely distorted; I thought I heard a curlew and the cry made my skin crawl. The pixies were going to get me, if the Wisht Hounds didn't first. It was almost preferable to break my neck stumbling through the clitter, or to fall into a bog and drown. I hugged my arms to my chest and thought, be calm, the fog will lift in a minute. But it didn't. It got worse. A howling wind tore at my hat and pellets of hail whipped in my face.

What would the intrepid Tommy Price do in a situation like this? Once, I remembered, she had run out of gas in Greenland and had to walk for hours through a blazing white landscape without markers. She had kept her spirits up by singing Noel Coward tunes. I tried one in a quavering voice. In reality I wasn't much good with nature adventures. I was used to taking care of myself in awkward, unfamiliar, and even dangerous situations involving people, but weather was another matter. Weather was *serious*.

Still, thinking of Tommy Price helped a little. I flattened my body against the side of the tor and began to inch around its circumference. The cold granite scraped my face but at last I found what I had vaguely recalled: a slit in the rock wide enough for a body to squeeze into. I don't know how long I sheltered there, but I had plenty of time to regret large portions of my life, particularly the portion that had begun yesterday with my arrival in Sticklecombe-in-the-Moor. I assumed that if I stayed here long enough, a search party would be sent out for me. Possibly Mrs. Droppington, seeing the fog sweep over the moors, had already alerted the search and rescue mission.

I may have dozed a little; at least I thought I was dreaming when I sensed a lull in the wind and a slight thinning of the fog. It wasn't complete, but still, looking out from my crack in the tor I realized I could see boulders, and the path, and some furze bushes. That was enough for me; if I didn't get moving I would freeze to death—my fingers inside my gloves were already like ice. I charged down the path, hoping that by always going down I would find my way back to the valley. I couldn't see any markers, couldn't remember how many paths there had been. The landscape seemed completely changed; no longer did the moor seem a bracing plateau with bones of granite jutting up through the thin soil. It was a swampy, squishy morass of pea-green bogs and pools that I could only avoid sometimes by jumping from tussock to tussock.

Still, even if I was chilled to the marrow, haunted by the thought of vicious pixies, and terribly, hopelessly lost, the fog *was* lifting.

If it hadn't lifted I doubt that I would have seen what I did: a tweed cap floating on a pool of green scum, and just underneath, the outlines of a woman's body, face down.

The coroner ruled the death of Tommy Price accidental. Everyone knew Miss Price's predilection for walking on the moors in every kind of weather. People did drown in the bogs—not often, but within memory. She was eighty-something after all and not as clear-headed as she could have been.

I returned to London with a violent cold and horrible memories of my headlong flight down the hill and into the first cottage I saw. The search party had no difficulty finding Tommy Price in spite of my incoherent directions; apparently she had stumbled into a well-known bog, not deep but treacherous all the same. More than a few ponies had lost their footing there and tired themselves out trying to get free.

I returned to London but I could not stop thinking about Tommy Price and Constance Root. Had it been Tommy who drove past me so quickly in the car? Why had Miss Root said Tommy was going to Burma when she was only out on the moors for a walk? That disapproval Miss Root had worn so plainly on her wrinkled face—was that envy? Or hatred? Perhaps she was jealous that Tommy Price's books were appearing in print again, that she was receiving public attention. But could she have been envious enough to kill Tommy? Would a woman in her eighties have the strength to push Tommy into a bog? And how had she gotten her up there in the first place?

Of course the oddest thing was that when the constable came to Tommy Price's cottage to inform Miss Root of the sad news, she was not in. A note pinned to the back door cancelled her milk delivery for an indefinite time. The car was gone.

"And she never came back," said Mrs. Droppington when I called a week later. "It's created an awful confusion here. You see Miss Price left everything to Miss Root in her will, just like Miss Root left everything to Miss Price. Who's going to get it if Miss Root doesn't come back? I'm over there watering the plants every other day, but I can't do that forever."

I had a sudden image of Constance strolling among the golden pagodas of upper Burma. Could she have decided to do away with Tommy and to steal her plane ticket? The likeliest way for Tommy to enter Burma was to fly from London to Calcutta or Bangkok, then to switch to a smaller plane and fly on to Rangoon. A few phone calls told me that a Miss Constance Root, not a Miss Edith Price, had booked a roundtrip ticket with Air India to Calcutta on December 2nd, but that she hadn't used it.

That didn't mean that Miss Root hadn't murdered Tommy Price and taken quite a different flight. Perhaps Miss Root *had* been planning to flee to Burma after the murder and only my unlooked for arrival had stopped her. However, for someone who had just murdered a woman and was preparing to escape to Burma, Miss Root had not seemed particularly agitated during my visit. Cold-bloodedness was much more likely to be a characteristic of Tommy Price than of Constance Root.

I recalled a favorite passage from *To the Top of the Very Top*:

"James lay there, stiff as a corpse on a mortuary slab.

"'Frozen, poor old sod,' I said to my companions.

"They were silent, struck with icy horror—James was the first of our party to die—who would be next?

"'Well, don't just stand there,' I said gruffly. 'We'll never get him down the mountain. We'll have to bury him here, in the snow, on the side of Mount Ktchnqhtl. Yes, he'd like that, I know. James was a brave chap, a climber till the end.'"

Yes, it seemed far more plausible that Tommy Price, with her nerves of steel and her tough, resilient old body hardened by years of trekking, sailing and camel-riding, would be able to kill fragile Miss Root. But the motives for such a murder seemed even less clear. Why would Tommy, basking in the fame of rediscovery, decide to bump off her old companion, who perhaps had been her lover once, or at least a good friend? Were there tensions between them that Tommy's sudden return to notoriety had inflamed? But if so, why didn't Tommy, with her vast acquaintance around the world, just leave? Why *didn't* she take that trip to Pagan?

I kept remembering the tweed cap floating on the green scum of the bog. After evading bandits and mercenaries and surviving frostbite and shipwrecks, what an inglorious end, to die face down in a pool of water.

It struck me as a curious thing that I couldn't remember ever seeing a photograph of Tommy Price. Not in any of her books, not in the interviews that had recently been published. I called up an editor I knew at Harridan Press, which was reprinting Tommy's travel books, and asked Jane if she had an author photograph.

"My dear," said Jane, "I never even *met* Tommy Price. We

corresponded by letter and the odd phone call. She said her health was too bad to come to London, that she never travelled any more."

"What did her voice sound like?"

"Nothing special, rather low and pleasant, not particularly quavery, if you know what I mean."

That was Constance's voice all right; but it could also have been Tommy Price's.

"What's this all about, anyway?" asked Jane.

"Oh, just curiosity, I suppose. I was supposed to meet her, but it didn't work out. I'm sorry, that's all."

"Well, I think she had a dashed good pop-off," said Jane. "Terribly dramatic, don't you think, to sink like a stone into a bog on Dartmoor? We're changing the back cover copy on the next two reprints."

I went to the British Library and found all Tommy's books. Not a single one had a photograph inside or out, though there were plenty of drawings of Tommy in burnooses, chaps and snow parkas with fur around the face. I couldn't help being struck as I flipped through the different volumes, how very many disguises she had taken on. Perhaps that's why she didn't want her photograph taken.

Or perhaps there was another reason.

I called up Mrs. Droppington again.

"This might seem an odd question, Mrs. Droppington, but did you ever actually *see* Tommy Price?"

"Of course. What do you mean? That is, when she was at the cottage, which wasn't very often, that is, I suppose she was gone for stretches at a time, that is, I do remember seeing photographs of her as a girl when her brother lived in the cottage."

There was a lengthy pause, and then Mrs. Droppington said thoughtfully, "Do you know, my dear, you've set me thinking. It's a curious thing, but I am really not so sure after all that I did ever see Tommy Price all that much. Ever since Tommy took over the cottage and Constance came to stay, I suppose it's Constance I've seen. I knew from what Constance said that Tommy was often travelling. Constance would come into the green grocers and say, "'Tommy's just back from Tanzania and says she absolutely must have sprouts for luncheon.'"

"But you couldn't exactly say what Tommy Price looked

like?"

"I often saw her from a distance," said Mrs. Droppington. "Tommy loved to walk, you know. She was always striding off across the moors, with her cap and walking stick. Quite a distinctive walk," Mrs. Droppington went on, gaining confidence. "Not at all like Miss Root's which was so . . . feminine."

I had a theory, which might be hard to prove, that Constance Root and Tommy Price were the same woman. That Tommy Price, with her love of disguise, had invented a kind of alter ego in Miss Root. After all, the two of them hadn't moved here until the 1970s, some years after Tommy Price's books had gone out of print. I imagined Tommy to be a proud woman, one who would find it difficult to admit that because of age and money she could no longer travel so easily, nor, if she did, write about it in a way that anyone would find interesting. She didn't want to retire as Tommy Price and have people say that she used to be a famous traveller, so she came up with Constance Root, a proper English lady, who could live on very little and still, with her stories of Tommy Price's adventures, keep her past myth alive. When the books began to be reissued, Tommy Price must have been thrilled at first, and then increasingly worried that her secret would be revealed. Hence the ban on photographs. She didn't want anyone from the village seeing the face of Tommy Price and saying, "But isn't that our Miss Root from Sticklecombe-in-the-Moor?"

The strain must have been too much for her and she had decided to do away with herself. Which is why no one had seen Constance after Tommy's death and why the plane ticket hadn't been used.

Of course such a theory had its soft spots, and why the camera-shy, reclusive Tommy had invited me to Dartmoor on the day before her suicide was the largest of them.

I travelled to Sticklecombe-in-the-Moor in the same way as before, by train to Exeter and then by hired car to the village. But this time I came very late at night. I parked my car in the village, and, all in black, with only a flashlight, I walked quickly to the familiar cottage.

The wind whistled through the moonlit night and it was absolutely silent. I tried not to think about Wisht Hounds and pixies.

With tools I had borrowed from a friend in London whose East End family dabbled in the burglary trade, I let myself into the front door of the cottage.

It looked the same as it had two weeks ago when I had visited; the same old-fashioned furniture, dustier now, the same book-lined sitting room, illumined through the windows by moonlight. I went into the sitting room and let my flashlight play along the spines of all those wonderful old titles. Tommy Price hadn't been the only woman writing books in the '30s; there had been Olive Chapman with *Across Lapland with Sledge* and *Reindeer*, Rosita Forbes with *Unconducted Wanderers* and *Adventure: Being a Gipsy Salad: Some Incidents, Excitements and Impressions of Twelve Highly-Seasoned Years*. I wondered what had happened to those writers. I knew that sometimes a traveller only took one huge trip and then retired in triumph to dine off stories of savages or sultans forever, and that sometimes she kept going, year after year, like Freya Stark and Dervla Murphy, drawn to hardship and adventure long past the age when most women were settling down to cro-cheting and gardening. What a shame that Tommy Price hadn't had the courage to admit to her double life. She was never going to enjoy the acclaim now that she so richly deserved. I couldn't help taking down the volume of *Bound for Greenland*. I had al-ways loved its description of the end of the voyage. Softly I read aloud:

"I always considered myself a seaman of the first order and it never occurred to me that my experience of the sea had been confined to tranquil oceans further south, azure and emerald play-grounds for dolphins and humpback whales. This was a sea of ice floes enormous as New York skyscrapers and vast swells the size of Himalayan mountains. Our ship had buckled and almost broken more than once; everything on the decks not tied down had been swept away and shards of glass and ceramic littered the galley where the cupboards had been forced open. But now it was over, now the small band of us stood on the deck, on the mercifully horizontal deck, as Greenland, great Greenland, land of Eskimos and Vikings, land of ice mountains and majestic peoples came into view. Thank God we were approaching land. At last."

"I always rather liked that passage myself," said a voice from the hall, a low, pleasant voice, not at all quavery.

I was so stunned I dropped the book and flashed my light

every way but the right way.

"I wrote it, you know," the voice continued. "I wrote all those books. We thought it was a lark at first, Tommy and I. We would go to the British Library and look up information, or we'd talk to people who really had been to those places. Then we'd go back to our small flat in Bayswater and I'd use all my powers of imagination. It was a lark, but it also paid the bills. Times were hard then."

"So you've never been to any of these places?" I sat down in a lump on the sofa, hardly able to take it in.

Constance Root advanced into the sitting room and sat down opposite me. The moonlight gave the room an unearthly cast but I could see her clearly. Her thin face was tired, yet I noticed she was wearing trousers and a heavy sweater and looked stronger than I remembered.

"We were poor as church mice, how could we travel?"

"Why did you use just Tommy's name?"

"My family was more respectable than Tommy's, you see. My father was a vicar in Somerset, I had five brothers and sisters. They never would have let me go off to Australia on my own, much less Greenland. Tommy just had her brother, who retired from his job in Exeter to Sticklecombe-in-the-Moor. He was much older than Tommy and thought she was rather wild and boyish. It seemed perfectly plausible to him that his sister would spend all her time exploring foreign places."

I was still trying to take it in. "And your publishers? Didn't they ever check?"

"You must remember, my dear, that in those days there was no television and rather less general knowledge of what places looked like. Tommy found she loved acting the part of intrepid explorer, and our publishers loved it, too. Periodically she'd dress up in khaki and tall leather boots with a riding jacket and a man's hat and swagger into the staid old office of Chatham and Bros. with a new manuscript. She refused to have her photograph in the books, and, on my suggestion, said she always travelled incognito, in disguise. That was to prevent people in the countries we wrote about from realizing that she had never been there."

"But after the books were successful, didn't you have any desire to actually travel to foreign places?"

"Tommy did," said Constance. "But my thought was that neither of us would be able to take the kind of chances I took in the travel books, and that if by any chance we were exposed, it would mean the end of a rather lucrative career."

"I thought for a while that you and Tommy Price were the same person," I said slowly. "And that Tommy had created you as a kind of alter ego, someone to stay at home while she explored the world."

"You could just as easily say that I created Tommy Price as my alter ego," Constance said. "Someone to explore the world for me while I stayed home."

My eyes went to the shelves of books in their faded bindings. How many happy days I'd passed reading about Tommy Price's adventures. And now it turned out they were bogus.

"It must have been hard for you when the books began to be reprinted," I said. "And suddenly the world discovered Tommy Price again."

"Things had not gone so well with us in the last twenty years," Constance said, with lips pinched. "Tommy was always such a demanding girl. It was as if she had come to believe my stories about her. She spent most of her time walking over the moors and expected me to wait on her hand and foot. It was easier to keep up the pretension that she still travelled a great deal. She wanted so much for the villagers to think so that she stayed inside for weeks at a time, and told me to give out that she was on a trip. When the books began to be reprinted, at first I was happy, for it would be more income. But then I realized what it was going to be like living with her."

"Now you have the income, but no Tommy Price to worry you," I said. "I know she left everything to you in the will."

"Yes, she did," said Constance equably.

"I'm curious about one thing," I said. "Why Tommy invited me here to visit?"

"I didn't know she had until you turned up. It was rather unexpected, to say the least." Constance's face looked quite ghostly now, and evil, as if she were a Dartmoor pixie come back in human shape. No time to turn my jacket inside out now, either. "Perhaps Tommy had begun to be afraid of me and wanted a witness," Constance said, so cold-bloodedly that I couldn't help shivering. I remembered the toughness of her books. She hasn't hesitated to shoot imaginary tigers or draw her gun against rampaging kangaroos, why would she stop at murder?

"And that ticket to Burma?"

"I bought it for myself, as a kind of reward, I suppose. But when I arrived at Heathrow on December 2nd, I realized that such a trip was impossible for me. The years when I could have enjoyed it were long over. I passed two not very agreeable weeks at a bed and breakfast in Bournemouth and returned home earlier tonight. I'll spend the rest of my life here"—Constance's mouth twisted, ironically or cruelly, I couldn't tell—"answering fan mail for Tommy."

"And when did you push Tommy into the bog and hold her down? Was she drugged? Was the car that passed me the afternoon of the 1st your car and were you driving her unconscious body to the moor and the bog? How did you manage it?"

"My dear Cassandra," Constance said distantly. "Tommy Price's death was accidental, as the coroner ruled. Everyone knows that Tommy loved the moors, and that the ground can be treacherously unstable. Why don't we just say that Tommy Price had the death she deserved: quick and dramatic."

"I think I had better tell someone," I said.

"No, you won't, my dear. You won't be believed, you know. Leave it as it is, and you'll be far more comfortable. You're only a tourist to the land of murder and I, after all this time, am now a traveller there."

Contributors' Notes

BRENDA MELTON BURNHAM is a former newspaper columnist for the *Chinook Observer*. She has been published in *Alfred Hitchcock's Mystery Magazine* and has won awards for her fiction and journalism. Her first Rocky Falls story appeared in *The Third WomanSleuth Anthology*.

HELEN and **LORRI CARPENTER**, a mother/daughter writing team, live and work in central Florida. Mysteries featuring their septuagenarian sleuth, Emma Twiggs, have appeared in all of the previous *WomanSleuth* anthologies. They are currently writing short stories for children.

LINDA E. CLOPTON has won awards for both drama and short fiction, including selection in the 1986 PEN Syndicated Fiction Project. She has just completed a mystery novel and is working on a second novel and a play.

LEILA DAVIS is the author of *Lover Boy*, a young adult romance, and has had short stories and articles published in magazines in the U.S., Canada, Great Britain and Norway. She has completed a number of British mysteries featuring her character Superintendent Nowell, and is currently working on novels featuring Felicity Gaudett.

LINDA WEISER FRIEDMAN is an associate professor of statistics and computer information systems at Baruch College of the City University of New York. She has published over forty articles in scholarly journals, as well as a textbook, *Comparative Programming Languages*. She is the co-author of a private-eye novel, *Deadly Stakes*. "If Wishes Could Kill" is her first published short story.

SALLY MILLER GEARHART has taught speech and drama for thirty-eight years, written a feminist utopian novel *The Wanderground*, and appeared as an activist in two documentaries about lesbians and gay men *Word Is Out* and *The Times of Harvey Milk*.

ROSE MILLION HEALEY lives and works in Manhattan, as does her fictional detective, Thelma Ade. Thelma has appeared in *Alfred Hitchcock's Mystery Magazine* and in the first and second *WomanSleuth* anthologies. Healey is currently working on a collection of Thelma's adventures.

NANCY R. HERNDON has published three novels under the pen name Elizabeth Chadwick: *Wanton Angel*, *Widow's Fire*, and *Virgin's Fire*. Her fourth, *Bride's Fire* will be published in 1992. She has had short stories published in *Women of the West*, *New Frontiers, II*, and *The Third WomanSleuth Anthology*.

JUDITH POST has published short stories in the first and third *WomanSleuth* anthologies. She's had mini-novels published by Penny Paper Novels and her work has appeared in *Byline* magazine. She is currently working on a full-length mystery novel.

EDIE RAMER has had short stories published in *Oui*, *Alfred Hitchcock's Mystery Magazine*, and *The Second WomanSleuth Anthology*. She has had a column published in *The West Bend News*. Her first writing sale was a humorous greeting card.

S. J. ROZAN is a practicing architect in New York City. In addition to her Lydia Chin stories, she writes about Bill Smith, Lydia's sometime-partner, and has just completed a novel involving them both.

CAROLINE STAFFORD's novels began appearing in 1974, and under various disguises she has enjoyed writing fiction and nonfiction ever since. Mrs. Dunlop made her debut in *The Third WomanSleuth Anthology*.

NAOMI STRICHARTZ was born in Brooklyn. She was a member of Ballet Russe de Monte Carlo and is currently directing the

Dance Circle Studio in Ithaca, New York. Previous Marya Cherkova stories appeared in the second and third *WomanSleuth* anthologies. She has written two children's books, *The Wisewoman* and *The Wisewoman's Sacred Wheel of the Year* (available from Cranehill Press, 708 Comfort Road, Spencer, N.Y. 14883).

LINDA WAGNER was born in New Jersey but has lived most of her life around Cleveland, Ohio. Earlier Livia Day Lewis stories appeared in the second and third *WomanSleuth* anthologies. She is currently working on a full-length mystery novel.

BARBARA WILSON is the author of three mysteries featuring Pam Nilsen and set in the Northwest, as well as the recently published *Gaudí Afternoon*, a Cassandra Reilly mystery that takes place in Barcelona. She is a co-publisher of Seal Press, which celebrates its 15th anniversary this year.

IRENE ZAHAVA (Editor) has compiled fifteen anthologies of women's writings including *Through Other Eyes: Animal Stories by Women*, *My Father's Daughter*, and *My Mother's Daughter*.